WHAT THE REVIEWERS SAY

"In all soberness, this book should be read by every American as we must look from Pearl Harbor ahead."

New York *Times Book Review*

"Here it is, right from the lips of the officers, fighting men, nurses, surgeons, chaplains, and civilians. It is a story of desperate courage and death, of feats of bravery far above the call of duty."

Philadelphia *Record*

"A book you won't put down, not even for dinner."

Los Angeles *Times*

"You hold on to *Remember Pearl Harbor!* with the left hand, while the right hand gropes for a gun. . . . A well-rounded picture, worthy of its monumental assignment."

New York *Daily Mirror*

"The words in this little book burn into the mind. They make one gloriously proud of the cool, daring, and brave American boys.

"The farther *Remember Pearl Harbor!* is spread throughout the nation and its Army and Navy, the greater will be the inspiration it gives. . . . I doubt whether any writer during this whole war will put the spirit of America in battle between covers more effectively."

Infantry Journal

D0017149

REMEMBER PEARL HARBOR

By BLAKE CLARK

revised edition
with
historical notes
by
Daniel Martinez

MUTUAL PUBLISHING
TALES OF THE PACIFIC
PAPERBACK SERIES
HONOLULU • HAWAII

Printed in Australia by The Book Printer, Victoria

For a complete listing of other books in the "Tales of the Pacific" series and ordering information, write to:

Mutual Publishing Company
2055 N. King Street
Honolulu, Hawaii 96819

Phone: (808) 924-7732

Cover photo by Doug Peebles

THIS BOOK CONTAINS THE COMPLETE TEXT
OF THE ORIGINAL HARDBOUND EDITION

Reader's Note: Chapter divider pages appearing in the original edition have been omitted to allow inclusion of additional material. This may cause gaps in page numbering.

TO THE
HEROIC DEFENDERS
OF WAKE

☆

ACKNOWLEDGMENTS

My greatest aid in telling the story of the battle at Pearl Harbor came from the scores of officers, chaplains, nurses, and fighting men whose individual stories combine into the single narrative. Many of these persons are named in the book. Many are not, for reasons of their own. I thank them all.

CONTENTS

ILLUSTRATIONS

*These illustrations, grouped as a separate section,
will be found following page 6*

12. The destroyer *Shaw*, in drydock, was literally cut in two. One side of the drydock (at right) went down; the other listed heavily.

13. Sailors disregarded the dangerous possibilities of explosions and manned boats close to the side of the burning U.S.S. *West Virginia*. The American flag showed clear against the smoke-blackened sky.

14. The quick-thinking Captain steamed out of the channel with the *Nevada* and grounded her where the Japanese could not sink her and bottle up the rest of the fleet.

15. Small boats rescued seamen from the U.S.S. *West Virginia*, which settled until her guns were ready to go under water. Men were still on board after smoke and flames reached the superstructure.

16. Burning oil streaming from shattered fuel tanks turned parts of the harbor into a sea of flame.

17. Men in boats from the damaged *Maryland* helped rescue survivors from the hull of the capsized *Oklahoma*.

18. The *Pennsylvania* was damaged slightly; the *Downes* and *Cassin* were a jumbled mass of wreckage.

19. Seamen swarmed to "abandon ship" as the *California* listed and settled on the bottom of the harbor.

20. Today big guns guard a Hawaii more powerful than ever before.

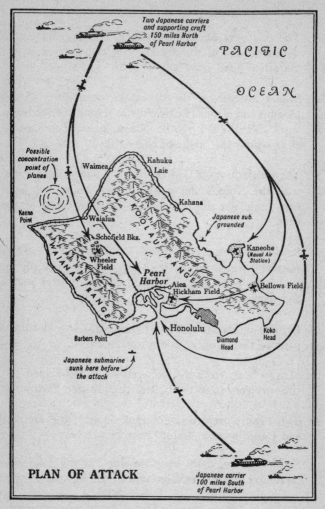

Two Japanese carriers
and supporting craft
150 miles North
of Pearl Harbor

PACIFIC

OCEAN

Possible
concentration
point of
planes

Kaena
Point

Waimea

Kahuku
Laie

Kahana

Japanese sub.
grounded

Waialua

Schofield Bks.

KOOLAU RANGE

Wheeler
Field

WAIANAE RANGE

Kaneohe
(Naval Air
Station)

Pearl
Harbor

Aiea
Hickham Field

Bellows Field

Barbers Point

Honolulu

Japanese submarine
sunk here before
the attack

Diamond
Head

Koko
Head

PLAN OF ATTACK

Japanese carrier
100 miles South
of Pearl Harbor

*See Chapter XIV: Historical Notes.

I

THIS IS HONOLULU

ALL MY LIFE I HAVE WANTED TO LIVE HISTORY. I would feel cheated indeed if I had lived through the age of Napoleon and not seen at first hand the Paris mob, the march to Moscow, or the Battle of Waterloo. Ever since I read the book, I have envied John Reed and Boardman Robinson the ten days that shook the world. I should like to have been in Europe during the First World War. I do not crave sensation, nor dream of a life of adventure. I never envied Richard Halliburton's individualistic exploits.* What I have wanted is simply to be present when significant history is in the making.

I have had my wish. I have been very close to some of the horrors and glories of one of the most crucial battles in America's history. I did not see it all with

*See Chapter XIV: Historical Notes.

my own eyes. I was not everywhere at once, as all men would have liked to be—at Hickam Field manning an anti-aircraft gun, in a pursuit plane fighting off Japanese bombers over Pearl Harbor, in a motor car racing out to Tripler Hospital with blood plasma. But from what I did see with my own eyes and from talking to friends and others who were in all the different centers of action "when it happened," I have lived through real history—the history of Pearl Harbor. Its beginning is as calm as the South Seas, and its ending is as angry and determined as the U. S. Marines who cry for revenge of Wake Island.

Honolulu is one of the calmest, sunniest, most delightfully peaceful cities in the world. Its name means "Fair Haven," and a fair haven it has been to millions of people in the course of its history. Sundays are especially quiet here. It is like a small New England town. Cars hardly start moving before ten o'clock. We have late breakfasts; then the young are off to the beach, the old to church. On that particular Sunday it seemed more peaceful than usual. The broad Pacific washed upon the shores of Oahu so gently that the Waikiki waves were too small to attract early Sunday surfers. There were so few clouds that the top of Mount Tantalus behind the city showed more than clear against the sky.

Most of us were just getting out of bed or having breakfast when the shooting started. I heard the rumbling noise of coast artillery practice, as I thought, and came on down to read the Sunday *Advertiser* before breakfast. Our copy had not come. It was the first time I had ever known it not to be there. When I walked down to Blackshear's drug store around the corner, the druggist smiled as I picked up the last copy and said, "Nobody got their paper this morning. Heard the presses broke down. This is an early edition."

Mr. and Mrs. Frear, with whom I am living on Punahou Street, were already seated when I came back. I gave Mr. Frear the paper, and he read "the juicy bits" to us as we ate our waffles and bacon. Divorces were very numerous in Honolulu now, he read. "All a woman has to do to get a divorce these days is say her husband doesn't keep his shirt clean," he observed, smiling at himself for the reactionary remark. Looking back at the paper, he read that we should send safety razor blades to the British soldiers, because steel was short now, and nothing helped a Tommy's morale like a clean shave. The rumbling outside continued.

Yamato came running in. "Plenty plane outside!" he exclaimed. "Come see!"

Led by the little Japanese, we went to the back porch. We could see a squadron of planes high above. Over Pearl Harbor we saw the sky dotted with black puffs of anti-aircraft smoke, hanging heavily in the air.

"That's good," said Mr. Frear. "We *ought* to get ready."

Miss Claire, our neighbor, who has retired from Punahou School where she taught the town's grandparents, parents, and children, came running through the house.

"We're under attack! The Japanese are bombing Oahu!" she said, looking apologetically at Yamato and his rotund little wife Hatsu.

"Oh, no, it's only practice. Don't get excited, Claire," said Mr. Frear, and we all chimed in reassuringly. Poor Miss Claire retired, convinced she had been the victim of rumor.

In a few minutes she had her revenge, though not one which she relished. As we were finishing our breakfast, we saw her again running across the lawn.

"If you don't believe it, turn on your radio!" she exclaimed as she came in.

I clicked the dial. "Keep calm, everybody. Oahu is under attack. This is no joke. It's the real McCoy. The emblem of the Rising Sun has been seen on the

1. Aerial bombs blasted Kaneohe Naval Air Base, leaving the airport pock-marked with craters.

2. The Japanese strafed and bombed rows of tents at Wheeler Field.

3. Seamen at Kaneohe Naval Air Station placed Hawaiian flower leis on the graves of their fellow sailors.

4. Firemen rushed to fight oil fires that flamed up at Hickam Field.

5. The crew of the U.S.S. *Ward's* number three gun fired the first shot of the battle of Pearl Harbor and sank an enemy submarine.

6. The General's staff car was riddled at Wheeler Field.

7. The minelayer *Oglala* capsized. Smoke poured from the *Helena*, the *Shaw*, and the *Maryland*.

8. The *West Virginia*, heavily hit, was settling; water poured from the *Tennessee*; the *Arizona* was down.

9. An oil tank at the Pearl Harbor Naval Air Station exploded in bursts of lemon-yellow flame and black smoke.

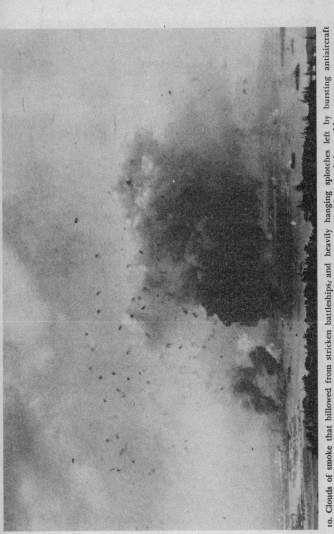

10. Clouds of smoke that billowed from stricken battleships, and heavily hanging splotches left by bursting antiaircraft shells made "the fullest wedge of sky" ever seen in this part of the world.

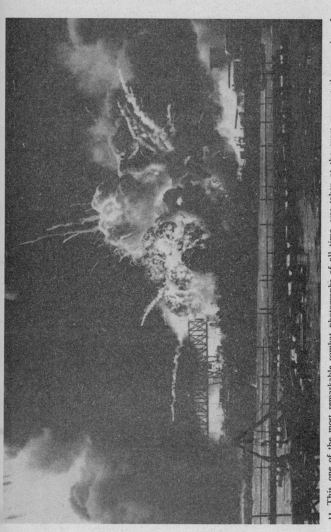

11. This, one of the most remarkable combat photographs of all time, was taken at the exact moment the magazine of the destroyer *Shaw* exploded.

12. The destroyer *Shaw*, in drydock, was literally cut in two . One side of the drydock (at right) went down; the other listed heavily.

13. Sailors disregarded the dangerous possibilities of explosions and manned boats close to the side of the burning U.S.S. *West Virginia*. The American flag showed clear against the smoke-blackened sky.

14. The quick-thinking Captain steamed out of the channel with the *Nevada* and grounded her where the Japanese could not sink her and bottle up the rest of the fleet.

15. Small boats rescued seamen from the U.S.S. *West Virginia*, which settled until her guns were ready to go under water. Men were still on board after smoke and flames reached the superstructure.

16. Burning oil streaming from shattered fuel tanks turned parts of the harbor into a sea of flame.

17. Men in boats from the damaged *Maryland* helped rescue survivors from the hull of the capsized *Oklahoma*.

18. The *Pennsylvania* was damaged slightly; the *Downes* and *Cassin* were a jumbled mass of wreckage.

19. Seamen swarmed to "abandon ship" as the *California* listed and settled on the bottom of the harbor.

20. Today big guns guard a Hawaii more powerful than ever before.

wings of the attacking planes." I recognized the dynamic voice of Webley Edwards, KGMB station manager.

The first thing I thought was "Hatsu and Yamato—what will they do?"

Yamato and Hatsu both are alien Japanese. Neither speaks English well. They subscribe to the Japanese paper here, and they have a good short-wave radio on which they pick up news broadcasts from Japan every night after they retire to the servants' quarters at the rear of the lawn. Their seventeen-year-old son, Shigeru, has just returned from Japan, where they sent him to be educated. Yamato is a very efficient little fellow. I would choose him to execute almost any kind of plan. I have insisted that the loyalty of the Japanese in Hawaii, the great majority at least, is unquestionable; but I confess that at the moment I became convinced of the attack, I had more hope than conviction that I had been right.

We called them from the kitchen and told them what the radio had announced.

Yamato smiled. "I don't think so," he said uncertainly.

Hatsu said, "No. They no fight. In Washington, Kurusu—you know Kurusu and Plesident still talk. No fight yet. Still talk." *

*See Chapter IV. Historical Notes.

As we gradually convinced them, Hatsu became physically ill. She and Mrs. Frear both cried, and they hugged each other, weeping, assuring each other that they understood, that no matter what happened they had been friends for years and would continue to be so in the years to come.

A light blue car turned into the driveway, bumped across the sidewalk, and came to a quick stop under the portico. A buxom little woman in Red Cross uniform ran up the steps. It was Mrs. Chandler, wife of the commander of one of the ships here. We had not recognized her at first in her Red Cross cap and gray dress.

"I'm bringing some girls from the ship here to spend the night," she announced. "They need to be near the maternity hospital down the street in case of emergency."

"What are you doing?" she said, turning to me. "Come on. I need a man to help me evacuate people."

I climbed in, and Mrs. Chandler shot out of the driveway.

I was on my way to my first taste of history in the making.

"We're going first to Mabel's," she said. "I'm checking with every woman connected with our ship and being sure they are taken care of, out of the danger zones, near the hospital if they are about to have babies."

"What's happened? How much damage is done? How many planes attacked? What's going on?" I asked.

"The Japs slipped in," she said. "Went right into Pearl Harbor."

And she went on to tell the damage that had been done—the flying fields attacked, the ships disabled, the smoke rising from Pearl Harbor, the oil burning on top of the water, men swimming in it, the hundreds of wounded being rushed to the hospitals, the death of Admiral Kidd.*"More damage in one hour than the U. S. fleet suffered in the entire World War! . . .

"They say two small subs got in the Harbor. I don't believe it. I don't believe they could get through. We don't know how it happened, but it's awful!"

We arrived at Mabel's on Pacific Heights. She had everything packed that she would need for several days. I carted it down, helped her and her little boy into the car. She told us about the bomb that struck the house a few doors below. It had torn away one whole end of the place, but had not harmed the dining room where the entire family were having breakfast. She and Mrs. Chandler wondered whether "their ship" was in the harbor and whether it was one of

*See Chapter XIV: Historical Notes.

those bombed. Mrs. Chandler's son-in-law, Bill, is a gunnery officer on the same ship.

"If Bill doesn't get one of those Jap carriers, I'll not let him in the house," she said.

All day long we drove through the streets.

Every few minutes we saw reminders of the attack. Driving along Kuhio Street at Waikiki, we came upon a house wrecked by a bomb which had exploded in the lawn. Even more sorrowful a spectacle than the house, I thought, was a coconut tree with its plumes blown off, leaving its strong, ugly stump staring at the sky. Across the canal, where McCully meets King Street, half a block of smoking, charred ruins were all that was left of the drug store where I used to buy my safety razor blades. It was completely wiped out, and, with it, the owner, his wife, and two girls who lived upstairs above the store.

On the lawn of Washington Place, the home of Governor Poindexter, a crowd of men stood looking into a wide hole left by a bomb. A photographer was taking a picture of a man standing shoulder deep in the bombpit, holding up a piece of shrapnel.

A dead Chinese man lay on the sidewalk near the shattered windows of the Schumann Carriage Company.

At the lower edge of Alewa Heights, there was a

gaping hole in the asphalt pavement. Children were running up the street to where a part-Hawaiian man was holding a limp young girl in his arms. The family of five had been standing on the doorstep when the bomb fell. A piece of shrapnel had flown straight to the girl's heart. The man looked helplessly about him for a moment, then ran up the steps of his home and disappeared into the house with his dead daughter.

On Judd Street, near Iolani School, a five-passenger automobile lay in a twisted wreck. Fragments of fenders and glass had been blown across the road. A direct hit from above had killed the four men who were riding in it. *

Bit by bit, we began to see what had happened. The Japanese, while their ambassador in Washington "still talk," had slipped up on the unsuspecting island under cover of darkness. Undoubtedly itching to drop their bombs on Pearl Harbor, their chief objective, and get away, they had first attacked each airport, bombing the hangars and mercilessly strafing the unprotected planes, lined up in orderly rows on the clean fields. Then, feeling relatively secure from pursuit and retaliation, they flew to Pearl Harbor and bombed the ships lying at anchor there.

We were quiet as we listened to each new story. We felt sick at our stomachs. Letting the damn Japs

*See Chapter XIV: Historical Notes.

slip in and throw our own scrap-iron back in our faces! Fortunately, we were too busy to feel helpless. Mrs. Chandler and, through her, the American Red Cross had us in tow. They knew there were things to be done, and they knew how to do them.

I began to feel better. I had a job to do, even though it was a small one—a grown-up man, following a woman around. In Kahala we passed Montgomery Clark and another fellow going from house to house, already on the job as fire wardens. "Have your garden hose ready for regular fire. Get a bucket of sand to throw on fires caused by incendiary bombs," they were telling residents of their districts.

"Not a big job, either," I thought, "but it's a very necessary one, and they're getting it done. Everybody's doing something."

That night, Mrs. Chandler's "ship's wives" properly accounted for to the last one, we clustered together, "fifteen of us—counting unborn babies—" as Mr. Frear said, sitting around the radio in the dark, asking each other questions which we could not answer.

"How did they do it? Did they get help from the local Japanese? Are the Hawaiian Japanese out sabotaging? Have parachute troops really landed in Woodlawn and Upper Manoa, as we heard? Do the Japanese have airplane carriers? Will more planes come back tonight? Will the searchers find the two Japanese airmen who bailed out over Barber's Point when American fighters shot their planes from under them? Now, the two enemies were stealthily searching a means of escape; but in a few hours would they not grow desperate for food and force their way into someone's home?" Coast guard and artillery troops armed with rifles and machine guns were searching for them. Then we heard that one of the Japanese men was killed. His companion had dragged him to the beach and buried him hastily, leaving his feet protruding from the sand. "Had the second Japanese been cornered? Were there other parachutists yet undiscovered, making their way through the lantana underbrush to break into blacked-out houses?"

We knew that volunteers had been out since noon to guard the strategic portion of shoreline at Kewalo basin. For years the scene of the coming and going of Japanese fishing sampans, that night the area was under special watch by civilians who had been issued Springfield rifles and assigned to their posts under command of an Army officer. All night they were to patrol the dark, rainy beach and adjacent areas, searching the sampan fleet for possible stowaways and peering into the dark waters of the Pacific for landing barges from

Japanese transports rumored to be five miles offshore. Edgar Rice Burroughs, James Humphreys, Anton Rost, and others—writers, businessmen, engineers, bartenders, and native Hawaiians were feverishly digging slit trenches in the blacked-out night, sweat and rain begriming their faces and soaking through their clothes. They had no time to think of sore muscles and aching backs, but only of the job to be done for the protection of their beloved islands.

At the Frears', as we each sought out our sleeping places, I realized that this had been the most stirring day in the history of Hawaii—and it has had some pretty glowing times. But I had seen and heard all too little. There were so many more things I wanted to know. My mind kept coming back to the Japanese. I remembered all the horror stories I had heard about yard men being prepared to cut off the heads of their employers. Absurd, but as I groped around in the dark I thought of Yamato and his efficiency. Ashamed to let anyone else know what I was thinking, I slipped downstairs and brought in the outside keys to the front and back doors.

I resolved to start the very next morning getting the story of what happened. I was going to talk to everybody I could who had seen the events of the day at first hand—to everyone from commanding officers on down to the lowliest seaman second-class, to the wounded, the unhurt, the heroes, and the anonymous workers whose collective response to duty was even more important than the feats of individuals, extraordinary as they were.

I got that story, and I shall never forget it. It was the most moving I had ever heard. Nothing I could add to what these American officers and men told me could make it better. If emotion is here, it is because these are the words of the many men who did the deeds of heroism and who uncomplainingly suffered the wounds and agonies. The figures of speech are theirs, the restraint, and the lack of desire for an "effect."

Theirs is a plain, straightforward story, but if I have told it as I have tried to—that is, as it was given to me—it will make every man in America want to shoulder a gun and every woman wish to be a soldier's wife in this war.

II

THE ATTACK BEGINS

"WE JUST HAVE TO ADMIT THAT THEY CAUGHT US with our *malos* down," a Naval officer remarked. [*] Formally, as all of us in Hawaii had reason to know, the Army and Navy were well warned, equipped, and rehearsed for an attack on the island of Oahu. In January, Admiral Husband Edward Kimmel, Commander-in-Chief of the Pacific Fleet, and General Walter Short, Commanding General of the Hawaiian Department, were advised by the Secretaries of Navy and Army that hostilities with Japan might easily begin with a surprise attack upon the fleet or the naval base at Pearl Harbor. This attack would most likely take the form of air bombing or air torpedoing, they were told. [*]

This information was not made public in the islands,

[*]See Chapter XIV: Historical Notes.

but we heard of it in the whir of hundreds of airplanes zooming low overhead, drowning out our classes at the University with their sudden hoarse roar. We saw that months before December 7th, Hawaiian skies were filled with planes and the warm Hawaiian waters with all kinds of ships playing joint Army and Navy war games with a grim purpose.

Nights brought powerful searchlights exploring the sky, impaling enemy airplanes on their beams and holding them like silver bees for all to see. Days brought artillery men firing away at moving tanks, men, and guns running on concealed tracks in one of the most expansive and complete practice fields ever known. In dramatic maneuvers the island was attacked and defended. In repeated military operations simulating real warfare as nearly as possible, the Army defenders of Oahu maintained an "inshore patrol" covering the circumference of the island to a distance of about twenty miles. Navy defenders, demonstrating their part in the joint coastal defense plan, made extensive reconnaissance flights, radiating as far as seven hundred miles out from Oahu.

As the date of the attack drew near, more radio warnings flashed to the Commanders:

"Negotiations with Japan seem to be ending."

"Japanese action is unpredictable."

"Hostilities on the part of Japan are momentarily possible."

During the first six days of December, the messages were more insistent, and demanded action:

"Destroy all codes; burn secret documents."

"Retain only such confidential material as is necessary."

The islands went on Alert Number One—against sabotage. Suspicious aliens were watched more carefully than ever. The submarine patrol was strengthened. But Alert Number Three—against attack by air, did not go into effect.

"M-Day may be closer than you think," a Naval officer remarked to his dinner partner at the Pacific Club on Saturday night, December 6th.

But the officer's Admiral apparently was not disturbed, nor was the Commanding General of the Hawaiian area. The General had received a final drastic warning of "impending hostile Japanese action." The Admiral had been told, "This dispatch is to be considered a war warning." Yet the two highest in command in the island outpost did not confer and put into effect the joint defense plans which we in Honolulu had so often seen rehearsed and in which everyone, civilian and service man, felt so much confidence.

In spite of the admitted dereliction of duty on the part of the high command, most of the holocaust of Pearl Harbor could probably have been averted and virtually all of Japan's attacking planes brought to earth in flaming wreckage but for three heartbreaking misses yet to follow. All occurred during the first hour before the attack, early Sunday morning.

At 6:50 A.M. the destroyer *Ward* was patrolling Pearl Harbor's entrance. Lieutenant Commander William Woodward Outerbridge, alert commander of the ship, detected the periscope of a Japanese submarine.

"Attack!" he ordered without hesitation. The submarine was in forbidden waters. The second shot from the destroyer's Number Three gun scored a direct hit. As oil and debris rose to the surface of the water, the *Ward* passed over the sinking submarine and completed its destruction with depth charges.

The first shot in the war of the Pacific was fired more than an hour before a Japanese bomb fell on Pearl Harbor.

Commander Outerbridge immediately radioed full details to headquarters, but no alert was called.* Since the joint defense plan had not been ordered into operation, neither the Army twenty-mile inshore patrol nor the seven-hundred mile Navy reconnais-

---

*See Chapter XIV: Historical Notes.

sance was on duty. Naval Intelligence had received no word that Japanese aircraft carriers were at sea, and so concluded that they were snug in home ports in far-off Japan.

At the moment Commander Outerbridge and his men smashed the enemy submarine at the mouth of the harbor, a second warning—a last minute emergency message—was on its way to the high command in Hawaii.

"An almost immediate break is expected between the United States and Japan," it warned. It was dispatched from Washington at noon, eastern standard time—6:30 A.M. Honolulu time. Although "every effort was made to have the message reach Hawaii in the briefest possible time," because of "conditions beyond the control of anyone concerned" it failed to do so, and thousands of America's fighting men were to die before the message was finally delivered.

Yet, incredibly, there was *still* time to avert disaster, and there came a third and final warning.

Private Joseph L. Lockard was listening in on one of the detector units which the Army had recently installed—an instrument so marvelously sensitive that it picks up the whir of an airplane motor more than a hundred miles away. Officially, the detector was closed at seven A.M.,* but in order to instruct another

*See Chapter XIV: Historical Notes.

soldier who was learning how to operate the unit, Private Lockard kept the instrument tuned in.

At exactly two minutes past seven o'clock, Lockard sensed that the detector had picked up something. His heart beat fast as he interpreted the signal: "Planes— lots of them—a hundred and thirty two miles distant." The excited private re-checked the distance. He re-checked the azimuth. Then he called the Army Information Center.

"Flash—planes—a hundred and thirty two miles— approaching from an unusual direction."

The vital message was quickly taken by a young lieutenant. It was not yet 7:20. The swiftly approaching planes were still thirty-five minutes away. Time to alert the island. Time to rouse the aviators at Wheeler, Hickam, Ford Island. Time for hundreds of American fighter planes to rise into the air to meet the invaders. Time for the call to General Quarters, to battle stations, for anti-aircraft guns to turn skyward, for ships to put up a barrage of fire that it would have been suicide to penetrate.

But the anonymous lieutenant at the Center had inside information—accurate information—that a delivery of American bombers was expected that morning from the mainland. He thought that the flight of planes which Private Lockard had detected was the covey of friendly bombers, and took no action on the message. *

The last chance for a military alert had come and gone. Unheralded, above the quiet Pacific the deadly Japanese bombers flew on, headed for an unsuspecting island.

The approaching planes doubtless came from three or four of Japan's smallest, fastest carriers, which had set out from the mandated islands and reached striking distance of Oahu.* In the darkness of the night they separated, two or three carriers proceeding two hundred miles to the north of the island and one coming in to the south. Then, in a great air pincer enclosing the entire island, blood spots of the Rising Sun gleaming on their wing tips, the unleashed war hawks swooped down for the kill.

The greater force from the north headed for the Naval Air base at Kaneohe and for Wheeler, Bellows, and Hickam airfields. Supporting squadrons from the south made for Honolulu and Hickam Field. They all met at Pearl Harbor.

*See Chapter XIV: Historical Notes.

III

AT THE FLYING FIELDS

KANEOHE

IT IS NO MILITARY OR NAVAL SECRET THAT OUR airfields on Oahu are here to protect Pearl Harbor, America's "billion-dollar fist" in the Pacific. Wheeler Field, Hickam Field, Bellows Field, the Naval Air Base at Kaneohe, the Marine Base at Ewa, were all built for a purpose and are an essential part of our defenses. All these are within quick flying time of the Harbor. Three are not more than two or three minutes apart when you are in a plane going three hundred miles an hour. Everyone knows this, and no one better than the Japanese who attacked on that fateful Sunday. They tried to ground every plane we had in order to prevent pursuit by our pilots.

The commanding officer of the Kaneohe Naval

Air Base was having his breakfast coffee, grunting an occasional "Uh-huh" to his fifteen-year-old son's remarks about Superman. The commander heard planes in the direction of the Koolau mountains. He looked out the window and saw four flights of three planes each, flying low, and making a right turn into the entrance of the bay, where planes of the naval air base were moored. *

"Those fools know there is a strict rule against making a right turn there!" the commander exclaimed, leaping to his feet.

His son said, "Look, red circles on the wings!"

The first alarm signal that Kaneohe received was the screeching of the commander's automobile tires coming down hill to the administration building, his battle station.

The Japanese planes shifted into echelon formation—a straight row, each plane slightly higher than its predecessor—as they zoomed over the quiet bay. They flew low, no more than fifty feet above the unruffled surface of the water. Below, four planes lay anchored in the bay. A hundred yards away the crews of the anchored airplanes were changing shifts. Two boat loads of young seamen were passing each other. "Here comes Tojo!" one of the boys joked. The Japanese opened up. Machine gun bullets spraying into

*See Chapter XIV: Historical Notes.

the water made a wide lane of geysers that led straight to the two boats and the anchored planes. Incendiary bullets and tracers shot down. Some bounced off the planes in red streaks. Some went through the anchored planes and sizzled in the water. The four planes went up in flames. A few of the boys escaped.

The Japanese flew on to the end of the bay, circled, describing the large bottom loop of a figure eight, and came back. They were met with the fire of a single machine gun. Aviation Chief Ordnance M. John W. Finn had rushed into the armory as soon as the strafing started. He brought out a Lewis machine gun, which is a field-type gun on a fork ready to be placed on any raised platform. He set it up on a covered tin garbage can, not caring that he was in an exposed section of a plane-parking ramp, took a lead of fifty to seventy-five feet on the plane, and started shooting. Suddenly feeling a rush of heat over his body, he realized that the Japanese machine gunner had hit him, but he kept on firing.

The enemy echelon went straight for the Catalinas and P B Y bombing planes on the ramp and strafed them mercilessly. Four years practice in flying over and bombing helpless Chinese cities had made experts of the Japanese killers. Shooting .30 calibre incendiary machine gun bullets and big .20 millimeter explosive machine gun shells, they hit everything in sight as they roared over the ramp. They continued to the entrance of the bay, made the small loop of the figure eight, and came back again. Heedless of the strafers, gun crews rushed out to groups of blazing planes on the ramp—planes in which gasoline was bursting into sheets of flame, and ammunition was exploding. They salvaged machine guns from the blazing planes and set them up outside. Streams of fire converged upon the attackers. For twenty minutes the strafing attack kept up, the line of planes zooming relentlessly up and down in the figure eight, crossing each time directly over the planes on the ramp. Our Catalinas and P B Y's got it going and coming. The attackers also found time to do a bit of incidental strafing of unprotected persons. They killed and wounded some civilians on the roadway. They blew the tires off the car of a major, returning with his wife and children from church.

At the height of the attack, Alice Spencer, civilian telephone supervisor, arrived at her post and relieved an enlisted man for combat duty. Explosive machine gun bullets ploughed through the walls of the administration building; shells burst and threw out flaming liquid. Calmly Miss Spencer operated her switchboard, keeping the wires open for vital messages. Beseiged men took heart from her courageous example.

During the lull which followed the attack, Kaneohe Naval Air Base was the scene of more and faster activity than it had ever had before. All automobiles were commandeered and driven hastily to staggered positions on the field so that if an enemy plane tried to land it would crash on a car. All anti-aircraft units were set in place. Civilian employees rushed to help put out fires and salvage burning planes. Electrical lines and water mains were repaired, so that the utilities of the station were out of commission only a short while. Contractors' men leaped to the seats of their bull-dozers and pushed flaming planes a safe distance away from the hangars.

Mechanics, yeomen, ordnance men, and seamen dashed for guns and shells. At one stowage room the the door was locked. A mechanic, Alfred Perucci, shot the lock off with a pistol, issued all the available arms and ammunition, and organized belting and supply crews.

Twenty minutes and the Japanese were back again from the north—eighteen of them this time, nine bombers and nine fighter planes. They headed for the hangars and what was left of the American aircraft. As they flew low they attacked the contractors' men on their bull-dozers. They strafed the men moving the automobiles. They shot bullets three-quarters of an inch thick into the hurrying people on the ramp. One of these bullets sank a foot deep into a reinforced concrete wall. It left a hole a sewer pipe could have gone through. Wounded people fell, but they did not cry out.

Many of our casualties were caused by the refusal of workers and fighters to take shelter. Angry men in white uniforms stood out in the open and shook their fists at the murderous pilots in the planes.

We had no American planes in the air to meet the Japanese. Even if there had been any undamaged aircraft left, we had never based fighter planes at Kaneohe—only the heavy Catalinas and P B Y's—and one old utility plane which the Japanese shot to pieces. But, whereas few shots were fired by the Americans during the first attack, they met the second wave with fire from every machine gun and rifle on the base. Everywhere our gallant fighters answered back, but the attackers were flying fast and were hard to hit. A gunner had no place but his shoulder on which to anchor his Browning air-cooled automatic. It was five times as heavy as a good shotgun, it kicked five times as hard, and it hit him fifty times in five seconds. He bounced around on it like a ping-pong ball tied to a paddle. He may not have hit a thing, but he was in there throwing lead.

Inside a burning hangar, Fred Llewellyn and Dale Lyons were issuing ammunition for machine guns. It was like working in a blast furnace, but they stayed on until blown from their post by a bomb explosion. Dale's left foot was severed; Fred lost an eye.

The Japanese dropped bombs weighing two hundred and fifty pounds, each carrying one hundred pounds of T N T. Four pounds of this most efficient of all explosives will hurl a twenty-five pound piece of lead a distance of ten miles. The attackers flew down until they were but two hundred feet above their objectives, dropped their deadly "eggs," then immediately pulled out of their dives. If they had come one hundred feet nearer to the ground they would have been destroyed by the concussion caused by the explosion of their own bombs.

One bomb just missed a hangar and fell on open ground. The concussion drew a row of riveted steel-sash windows three inches from a wall eighty yards away. Rivets fairly leapt from the wall. A hundred yards farther on the concussion knocked down Finn, the ordnance man, at his gun. Bomb after bomb fell until the administration grounds five hundred yards away were littered with splinters from one to five pounds in weight.

Finn was hit by Japanese strafers several times, but throughout both attacks he steadfastly continued to return the enemy fire. Now he enjoyed sweet revenge. Coming straight toward him, flying low, just clearing the telephone wires, was a Japanese in a single-seat pursuit plane, strafing after the bombers, protecting them from attack. Finn took less lead this time, caught the nose of the flying plane in his sights, pulled the trigger once, and pushed hard against the kicking gun, while it poured its burst of fifty bullets into the Japanese plane. Others were undoubtedly shooting at him too. Perhaps it was not Finn who got him. He didn't care. The important thing was that the plane crashed on a knoll of ground near the water. One wheel bounced through a house; the motor landed a quarter of a mile away.

Several men ran out to the crashed single-engined Mitsubishi. The Japanese pilot, a lieutenant in threadbare uniform, was crushed the instant the plane hit the ground. *

"Look at that propeller blade!" exclaimed one officer. "It's American!"

"No, it's not! It's stamped here—'Made in Japan.' "

"It's a perfect imitation!"

*See Chapter XIV: Historical Notes.

"These accessories aren't imitation—they're ours, all right!" The men felt sick as they stared at U.S. made instruments on the board.

"Here's the pilot's mascot-coin—it's made of nickle, but plugged!"

"Pipe the screwy belt!" A seaman disentangled a wide strip of silk from the wreckage. The band was dotted with orderly rows of tiny red stitches.

"That's a Japanese Good Luck belt. I've seen them before," said an officer. "It has a thousand stitches, each one taken by a different person."

"It's a lucky belt, all right," the seaman replied. "It's all in one piece, which is more than I can say for the pilot!"

BELLOWS

Captain Clarence Johnson and his friend, Lieutenant Paul C. Plybon, got up early on December 7th. It was only seven o'clock, but the Captain, in command of Company G at Bellows Field, had work to do. His men were out on sabotage guard, were on roving patrol, and were guarding battle installations.

Lt. Plybon—off duty—telephoned a friend at Hickam Field who was planning to come over for some swimming at Waimanalo. While phoning, Plybon heard the sound of a loud explosion come over the wire. "Something's happened! I'll call you back!" said his friend.

There was no call-back, and there was no swimming at Waimanalo that day.

Captain John P. Joyce, Officer of the Day, his chin covered with soapy lather, was in the Officer's Club shaving when he heard a plane overhead, and a burst of some fifty rounds of ammunition. He ran outside.

"A plane fired on the Dispensary, Sir," reported a non-com excitedly. "She hit the mess hall and the Casual Detachment tents, too! Private Brown of the Medical Detachment was hit in the leg!"

Then came an urgent telephone call from Hickam Field, "Hickam has just been attacked! Please dispatch all available fire-fighting equipment that you can spare to this Field at once!"

Some minutes later, a car dashed up. A marine officer stuck his head out and yelled,

"For Christ's sake, get your men out! The island's being attacked!"

Captain Johnson's bugler blew an alert.

Truck loads of men were just leaving to reinforce installations around Bellows and pilots were rushing out to their planes when a formation of nine Japanese attackers flew in at low altitude from the direction of Kaneohe, broke up into flights of three, and strafed the field from different directions. The guard, which was deploying along the road in front of Observations, and the personnel of the Casual Detachment fired on the planes.

Captain E. L. Duggan saw the Bellows aviators rush to counter-attack. Lt. George A. Whiteman took off. Just as he pulled up from the end of the runway, his plane burst into flames and crashed on the beach. Lt. Christensen was running to his plane. A Japanese strafer, flying low, shot and killed the American as his hand touched the cockpit door. Lt. Bishop was in the air alone. Three Jap Zeros closed in, shot him down. He landed in the water, and although wounded, he survived the crash.

In the meantime, the remaining six Zeros were strafing the field. One, shooting bullets at everything on the runway, zoomed toward a transformer station where Privates Hiyakaya and Gonsalves were on guard. The two American soldiers—one of Japanese, one of Portuguese descent—did not seek cover. Kneeling in the path of the Zero's fire, they took careful aim with their Browning automatic rifles and squeezed the triggers. The plane passed over their heads, smoke trailing from it. It flew on across the sand dunes, went out of control, and crashed into the ocean.

The attention of the attackers was caught by two objects which they strafed relentlessly. One was a gasoline servicing trailer, the other an observation plane—an O-49, painted silver. The silver plane was completely riddled. The trailer burst into fire. Its seams broke and flaming gasoline spurted out toward five government trucks and three privately owned automobiles parked nearby. Captain Joyce and two men leapt into the trucks and cars and drove them out of the danger zone. Despite their efforts two brand new trucks—one a week old, the other three days old, went up in smoke.

After less than fifteen minutes of strafing, the enemy planes re-formed into one flight and flew back out to sea towards Kaneohe. *

THE MARINE BASE, EWA

The Marine Base, Ewa, a new incompleted air base a couple of minutes by plane from Pearl Harbor, was attacked as viciously as if it were an armed fortress. The first wave of Japanese planes concentrated their fire on all aircraft on the ground. During the momentary lull which followed, marines rushed out and

*See Chapter XIV: Historical Notes.

dragged unburned planes off the runway. They mounted free machine guns on them. There was no concealment or protection for these planes, and they were plainly visible to the attackers, but volunteers rushed to man the mounted guns. The brief lull was followed by a second attack more vicious than the first. Wave after wave of strafing planes swept across the field. Cannon and machine-gun fire churned the ground around the planes, and this time bombs sought out what bullets might miss. Every plane was a target selected for special attack. Yet the men stuck to their guns, pouring a stream of fire at each Japanese plane as it dove past.

Private Turner and Sergeant Peters were firing fast from one of these quickly improvised posts. Turner calmly handed ammunition to Peters, the gunner. A bomb fell not more than ten yards from the plane. Still they fired. Three of the mustard-yellow attackers came at once, pouring their heavy fire into the lone plane.* Turner was struck by machine-gun bullets. He fell from the wing of the plane, mortally wounded . . .

Throughout the attack every man carried out his emergency duties, despite the heavy fire which the Japanese poured upon every corner and cranny of the field. The marines distributed the ammunition, cleaned and serviced the guns, made bombs ready for use, and

*See Chapter XIV: Historical Notes.

in every spare moment got in telling shots at the enemy. Moving vehicles were the special targets of Japanese attack, yet drivers of ammunition trucks and ambulances made their trips to every part of the field without looking first to see if the sky was clear. Usually it was not.

Technical Sergeant William Turnage alone set up and manned a free machine gun in the midst of the hottest fire of the first wave of attackers. A Japanese plane swooped toward him. He held his machine gun on the plane. Gasoline suddenly spurted in streams from a dozen holes. The plane changed its course, spun into the woods a short distance away, and crashed in flames.

The marines had a one-man fire truck. In the midst of the first attack driver Shaw spotted several planes that had been set afire by Japanese incendiary bullets. He climbed into his red fire truck and set out for the line to put out the fires. Strafers, attracted by the bright red truck, attacked before Shaw got half way to the planes. They riddled the truck with machine-gun fire. Shaw kept on. Two more planes attacked him. Still he drove. He did not stop until a third wave shot the tires off his wheels. When an officer commented drily upon his driving into a hail of machine-gun bullets, Shaw said, "Hell, Lieutenant, I saw a fire, and I'm supposed to put 'em out."

A master technical sergeant, veteran of the World War and the Nicaraguan campaign, was in charge of a bomb-handling detail. The attack became especially heavy in his area. He calmly devoted all his attention to the task at hand, ignoring the strafing with complete disdain.

"Sergeant! Take cover!" an officer yelled across to him.

"To hell with the cover!" he shouted back. "I'm fifty years old. Get the kids under cover!"

His bomb load went right on to the line of operation.

WHEELER

The Mikado's plans necessitated immediate attack on the Army's Wheeler Field. Named for World War I ace, Major Sheldon Wheeler, it based the fastest Army pursuit planes in the world. It was imperative that these planes must not leave the ground to fight against the Rising Sun.

As the forty-eight Japanese planes swept along the level valley from the carriers at sea, they found their targets in perfect position for attack. Orderly row after row of American planes were lined up, reflecting the tropic sunlight. They were arranged with mathematical precision in accordance with Alert Number One—against sabotage. Wing touched wing in close formation so that the precious planes could be effectively guarded. Alert Number Three—against attack by air, which calls for dispersion of grounded planes, had not been ordered. Diabolical luck was with the Japanese.

In the first few seconds of the attack, the Japanese destroyed probably forty planes, their gas tanks ignited by incendiary bullets or bombs. But the planes were not the only objects of Japanese devastation. Direct hits were scored on the power supply, the water supply, the telephone and radio communications, and the mess hall. At least one bomb left its scar on each important building on the Field. They hit an oil supply, and blue-black smoke, shot through with angry yellow flames, discolored the sky. Four hangars were reduced to burning embers. Machine gun bullets peppered the rows of tents nearby until they looked like canvas netting flapping in the wind.

The Japanese strafed and killed two Army flyers taking off, and another as he ran to his plane.

But the strategy of the attack on Wheeler Field was a failure. The Japanese surprised the Army pursuit pilots, but could not prevent some fifteen of them from getting into the air. These fifteen fighters made combat history.

Lieutenants George Welch and Kenneth Taylor, sitting at the officers' club at Wheeler, saw the enemy dive bombers swoop low over the ammunition hangar and drop their loads. Sinewy steel and thick bastions of concrete twisted and shattered at the high-power explosion. The lieutenants rushed outside, leaped into their car, and hit a hundred miles an hour on the way to a nearby airfield where they had their planes on special duty.* They did not stop to hear the size, number, or type of planes attacking, but grabbed their airplane orders from the interceptor control and dashed for their pursuit planes on the field.

They rose swiftly and at a height of a thousand feet saw a group of fifteen or twenty Japanese planes underneath them, strafing and bombing the airport, literally tearing it to pieces. The two Army lieutenants swept to attack. Welch made for a two-man dive bomber, a slow ship compared to his light craft. But as he sped towards his enemy, the Japanese rear-gunner saw him and began spraying lead in his direction. Welch pulled the trigger of one of his .50 caliber machine guns. It did not work! He tried the other. No response! It, too, was disconnected. By now he was rushing almost head-on into the Japanese plane. On his

*See Chapter XIV: Historical Notes.

left wing, a staccato row of holes appeared, each one nearer than the last to the cockpit. An incendiary bullet hit his plane and passed through the baggage compartment behind the seat.

He still had four .30 caliber guns, set to fire simultaneously. One jammed, but he pulled the trigger. The bullets from all three guns burst forth and the Japanese rear-gunner slumped forward over his gun. The enemy plane flopped over, smoke pouring out of the fuselage and circled to its final crash.

Welch climbed above the clouds and checked the damage to his plane. The incendiaries had not set it on fire. He dove through the clouds and returned to the air arena. A Japanese plane was flying out to sea. Welch caught it, shot it down with one well-aimed burst, and watched it fall into the broad Pacific below. Now his plane needed refueling. He headed back for Wheeler Field.

Lieutenant Taylor's plane overtook his first victim so fast that he had to throttle back to keep from overshooting. He found his mark and the plane went down. During his second attack, the enemy rear-gunner nicked Taylor's arm. The bullet spattered when it hit the seat, and a fragment pierced the American's leg. He felt it, but paid no attention to it. He joined

Welch in the return for refueling, and the two landed together.

Before Welch's guns could be serviced or Taylor's wounds receive first aid, a second wave of fifteen Japanese planes swept in, flying low, heading for the two planes on the runway. Taylor had been advised not to return to the air because of his wounds. He leaped to his plane, took off, rising at high speed, and turned in a perfectly executed chandelle. The Japanese were on his tail. Welch, in the air behind them, swept fast upon Taylor's pursuers and dove on the one most dangerous to his partner. The Japanese rear-gunner poured lead into Welch's plane. Bullets struck the motor, the propeller, the cowling. Still Welch pursued like an avenging fury, letting fly with all his guns. The enemy plane burst into flames and spiraled down. Taylor escaped. Welch followed another enemy plane seaward, caught it about five miles off-shore, and gave its two-man team an ocean grave.

This was Welch's fourth plane, brought down in his first battle flight, with more than half his normal shooting power out of action. Not even Eddie Rickenbacker ever shot down more than two planes in one engagement. Welch and Taylor were starting where the aces of World War I left off. And they were not alone.

Other squadrons were in the air. In another part of the sky Lieutenant Harry Brown saw his friend Lieutenant Robert Rogers in a dog-fight with two Japanese planes. Brown singled out the one on Rogers' tail and began shooting. He got nearer and nearer to the Japanese plane—so close that he could see his sharp-nosed tracers ploughing into it from the belly to the tail. One of his guns jammed. He pounded it with his fist until the skin burst. The plane in front started wobbling, then shot into flames and crashed into the sea. Brown's throat was sore and his voice hoarse from yelling during the excitement.

Lieutenant Sanders, called "Old-Man Sanders" by his fellow pilots because of his "extreme" age—thirty-four years, led a unit of four planes up through an overcast of six thousand feet. He saw a group of six Japanese bombing an airfield. He signaled his men to the attack, taking the enemy leader for himself. Although the sun was behind Sanders' unit, the Japanese saw them and fled north. The unit came in fast, dived on the Japanese, and started firing. Sanders opened up on the leader. The Japanese plane smoked up, faltered, and fell into the sea.

Lieutenant James Sterling was hot after one of the enemy. A second Japanese plane was on the American's tail. Lieutenant Sanders closed in on the rear enemy, but the attacker was already pouring bullets into Sterling's plane, and it burst into flames. Sterling continued to pour lead into the Japanese plane ahead, and the four went into a dive—the Japanese in front, Sterling still firing at him, the second Japanese after Sterling, and Sanders following through. They plunged down into the overcast at an altitude of six thousand feet, all motors roaring at full speed. Only Sanders pulled out.

Lieutenant Rasmussen was in a dog-fight with a Japanese over the pineapple fields of Wahiawa. Each was desperately maneuvering to get on the other's tail. Bullets flew into Rasmussen's plane. His radio equipment cracked to pieces before his eyes. The Japanese plane was fast, well-armed. Below, thousands of people who had evacuated their homes at Hickam and Ford Island, and thousands who had run outdoors at Schofield Barracks and Wahiawa stood anxiously watching the dog-fight, the most exciting form of modern warfare.

Rasmussen pulled up out of a fast maneuver. He caught the Japanese plane in his sights. He pulled the trigger of his .50 caliber machine gun. Tracer bullets ripped into the enemy plane. He held the deadly stream straight on the Japanese. When he quit firing, the plane was going down. The watching thousands broke into a great cheer of relief and pride when it fell to the ground in a burning, broken mass of wreckage.

When Rasmussen landed, he inspected his plane. The rudder had been completely shot away, and the fuselage was riddled by four hundred and fifty jagged holes.

The Japanese got full satisfaction from their visit to "the eagles of Wheeler." The Americans believed that if they had been given just ten minutes notice they could all have been aces. "It was like shooting fish in a barrel," Lieutenant Taylor said. The Japanese could not have foreseen it, but they had attacked Wheeler Field in flying-coffins. All of the pilots on the ground were frantic to take to the air to fight, but there were no more planes. Through blinding tears they watched those men take off whose planes were still intact. It was too much for one youth whose ship went up in flames before his eyes. He stole the squadron leader's plane and rose to battle before his superior could stop him.

On the ground men were running through dust clouds rising from the Japanese strafers' incendiary bullets that were ripping up the field. Demolition bombs were bursting on the hangars. Just before the explosions, Sergeant Bayham tore down to the supply house for a machine gun. He was breaking down a door when the supply sergeant, who was still thinking "practice," refused the gun and ammunition unless Bayham signed for it. By this time the door was down, and Bayham was dragging out a .50 caliber machine gun.

"I don't have time to sign for it!" he yelled.

When he finally mounted the gun, somebody cried out, "Hey, you can't fire that water-cooled gun without water!"

"To hell with the water—I haven't got any water!"

Staff Sergeant Benton joined him and fed the ammunition as Bayham pumped it at an approaching Japanese two-motored bomber. The gunner in the rear cockpit was shooting at them. Dirt popped up around them in small dust fountains. Their own tracer bullets told them that they were hitting the bomber. Ragged holes made a pattern on the fuselage and the cowling above the cockpit. When the plane had passed and was a couple of hundred yards away, it shook like a dog shaking off water, circled jerkily to the right, and fell.

Oahu's defenders fought. They fought on the sea, in the air, and wherever men found guns to fight with. Two Japanese planes came strafing the streets of

Wahiawa, a few miles from Wheeler Field. At the sound of firing, a lieutenant and a sergeant in charge of a communications section grabbed automatic rifles and rushed out to the sidewalk. The two planes flew low, slowly and deliberately. They raked everything in their path with machine gun fire. Puffs of dirt exploded as the bullets whipped into the earth. One plane, blazing away, swooped down toward the unprotected communications station. The Americans knelt, drew a bead on the plane as if aiming at a duck, calmly waited until it was within a hundred and fifty feet, and emptied their magazines. The machine guns stopped firing. The plane went out of control. It careened crazily sideways and crashed in flames a hundred yards behind the communications post.

Schofield Barracks, near Wahiawa, was virtually ignored by the Japanese except for a strange "bull's eye" that was reported. A machine gun bullet from an enemy plane pierced a tent where four cooks were playing cards. The bullet scored a direct hit on the pasteboards in the center of the table. The men, unhurt, sat there with their mouths open—staring at the punctured cards!

Hickam

Hickam Field, on December 7th the finest air corps station the United States Army could boast, lies so close to Pearl Harbor that from the air the two are virtually the same target. Its very position reveals its strategic military purpose—to protect the great Navy base. Only recently completed, its expanse of almost three thousand acres provided ample room for spacious landing fields, broad runways, and the hundreds of planes which called the giant hangars "home." Its futuristic concrete gates guarded a modern city carefully planned to clothe, house, and feed the thousands of Hickam workers and their families who lived at the Field.

Here, as at Wheeler, row after row of planes meticulously drawn up in Alert Number One parade formation awaited the Japanese hordes. They came in from the south in waves, bombing and strafing. High altitude bombers flying in V-formation, five to an echelon, carried one hundred to five hundred pound bombs.

A direct hit on a hangar announced the news of the attack to the thousands on the post. Men came pouring out from all nine wings of the barracks—men in slacks, men in shorts, some in their underwear only, some without anything on at all! Everyone dashed for his battle station.

Colonel Ferguson was in a building up the street from the hangar line. He ran out into the open, saw the damaged planes, and jumped into the gutter. While strafers bounced bullets off the road by his side, the Colonel crawled down the gutter to the line. There he directed the tactical squadrons who were arriving a hundred and fifty at a time on the double quick.

"Disperse those planes!" was the order.

The men hastened to execute the command, as up and back, up and back, the Japanese squadrons kept flying, strafing as they went. The Americans worked on, heedless of the rain of bullets. Some of the men faltered and fell.

A general's aide on the line tried to taxi one of the big bombers off the field. Strafers had put the left motor out of commission. It was no easy job to taxi such a heavy plane with only one motor going. He did it by racing the undamaged right engine until it pulled its side of the plane forward. Then he slammed on the opposite brake, forcing the left wing up. Crawfishing along under enemy fire, he brought the plane across the landing mat to comparative safety.

High altitude bombers dropped incendiaries and

high explosives on the cumbersome looking hangars, turning them to flame. Dive bombers darted in, dropping their twenty-five-pound "eggs" on the quarter-mile-long rows of planes, cutting many of them as squarely in two as if with a giant cleaver. Japanese pilots sailed just above the long rows of planes, pumping streams of incendiary machine gun bullets into those that the bombers failed to get. For a moment it seemed as if the incendiaries had done no damage. Then, one after another in quick succession, the grounded planes exploded in bursts of lemon-yellow flame, like huge fire-crackers at some monstrous Fourth of July celebration.

Sergeant Dwyer got a machine gun out of ordnance, put a corporal in charge of it, and dashed back for another. A bomb fell, scattering its deadly fragments. He got a second gun and set it up on the parade ground. He felt wet and looked at his shirt. It was soaked with blood. The sergeant remembered that something he had thought was a sharp stone had hit him when the bomb exploded. He was taken to the hospital with a shattered shoulder.

A lieutenant ran toward a plane. A Japanese flew over, strafing. The lieutenant fell to the ground, mortally wounded. A young corporal by his side lifted him to an ambulance, sped back across the apron, leaped to the plane, and taxied it out, finishing the job his buddy had started.

Corporal William Anderson, on duty as a radio operator, ran to the supply room and took a submachine gun. With utter disregard for his own safety, from the open field he shelled enemy strafers until—wounded many times—he died beside his gun.

Colonel Augustine Shea ran out of the supply building and headed for Operations Headquarters. He heard the screech of a bomb falling behind him and instantly thought "Martin!"

Sergeant Martin, one of the finest crew chiefs on the Field, had just gone into the supply building to get a new wheel to put on a bomber. The Colonel looked back in time to see the sergeant come out, rolling the fat wheel, when the bomb hit. Martin simply disappeared in the violent blast. Colonel Shea ran back to the supply building. Thousands of airplane parts—tires, wheels, nuts, bolts—all had been blown away. The place was as bare as if cleaned out by a cyclonic vacuum sweeper. Fortunately, it was Sunday, and the scores of secretaries, clerks, and stenographers were not at their desks.

Colonel Shea headed for the line. Men were scattering to get out of the way of a speeding truck which was carrying a four thousand gallon drum of gasoline.

The two drivers had been unloading a tanker when the attack began. At first, they had stuck to their seats on the theory that the truck could run faster than they could. But having dashed to comparative safety with one load of gasoline, they jumped from the truck and caught a return ride to the cargo ship to pick up another load. They leaped into another gasoline truck and speeded down the line to safety with it. Japanese were strafing continually. If only one incendiary bullet had pierced the gasoline drum, the men's bodies would never have been found. Yet they made their dangerous journey not one—but eight times! Not until they had successfully dispersed every loaded gasoline truck did the men abandon their perilous "round trips."

While the fire department fought flames at the tail end of some of the planes, daring crew men jumped up on the wings, disconnected the engines, and pulled their eight hundred pound precious metal burdens to the edge of the apron. Many fine engines were saved by their bravery and quick thinking.

The fire fighters were strafed as they worked. Chief W. J. Benedict was machine gunned until he fell, literally peppered with bullets, but miraculously, alive.

Six city fire fighting units joined the Hickam brigades and civilian and soldier fought flames side by side. Incendiary bullets rained piercing fire, gasoline exploded in sheets of consuming flame, but the men fought on.

Inside a hangar twenty-one Hawaiian fire fighters stood their ground. Planes roared hoarsely, machine guns stuttered overhead. In the middle of the smoke-filled hangar, Solomon Naauao, two hundred and forty-five pound athlete, trained the water from his fire-hose on the fuselage of a four-motored Flying Fortress, pushing back the gasoline flames that leaped out from the fuselage onto the wings. Solomon is a giant Hawaiian, a true son of a warrior. Short, thick, black hair fits his massive head like a fur cap. He was hoping the Chief would come soon with the foamite. Water was not much good against burning gasoline.

One end of the fire-weakened hangar fell through to the floor, revealing a sky dotted with three approaching Japanese bombers. They flew just a few feet above the hangar. The first one passed directly above Solomon and his fellow fighters. Solomon heard an explosion and felt hot pain.

"Lord help me!" he prayed, falling to the concrete floor. The whole inner side of his right leg was blown away.

Using his arms and sound leg he crawled through the smoke, away from the flames. Two soldiers carried him to the doorway to wait for the ambulance just coming in. As he lay there, Japanese planes flew slowly above, just clearing the hangar, and strafed the men running towards him to carry him to the ambulance. Others quickly lifted the wounded Hawaiian and sped him to the hospital.

Solomon Naauao's loyal companions stayed at their posts, though they were scorched by sudden bursts of flame, blasted by explosions, and shot down by machine guns. John Carreira, Thomas Samuel Macy, and Harry Tuck Lee Pang sacrificed their lives. Six others were severely wounded.*

Inside the Hickam guard house in the rear of the fire station sat a lone prisoner, a sergeant, condemned to prison and a dishonorable discharge from the Army. A guard rushed back and threw open the barred door.

"Come on!" he screamed. "This ain't maneuvers!"

The sergeant dashed to his battle station inside one of the hangars. An old-timer there, he directed rescue personnel so speedily and intelligently that he was credited with saving the lives of twenty persons trapped by white hot flames.

The "disgraced" sergeant is still in the Army—having traded his dishonorable discharge for a Distinguished Service Medal.

*See Chapter XIV: Historical Notes.

The raid lasted fifteen or twenty minutes. As soon as it ceased, activity burst upon the streets and flooded them. Ambulances and all cars that could be pressed into service as ambulances whizzed up to the bombed area and back. School buses, Army station wagons, American Factors delivery trucks, and private automobiles helped to deliver the wounded and to rush surgical supplies from Honolulu to the hospitals.

Before half their work was completed, Hickam was caught in the second and most destructive raid. Two straight lines of high-flying bombers dropped over twenty heavy and light demolition bombs from a height of ten to twelve thousand feet. They landed in the most populous section of the Field. For what seemed a full minute after the bombs had landed, there was a dead silence in which nothing happened. Then the new mess hall, large enough to lodge six complete basketball courts; the photograph laboratory; the guard house; the fire station; the barracks built to house thousands; an immense hangar—everything in the entire area—seemed to rise intact from the earth, poise in mid-air, and fall apart, dropping back to earth in millions of fragments and gigantic clouds of dust.*

The dust settled to reveal the third wave of Japanese strafers. Ground defenses were now going full

*See Chapter XIV: Historical Notes.

blast and accounted for several of the raiders. Guns were set up on the parade ground, on the hangar line, and even around the flagpole at post headquarters. One man—no one knows how—had lugged a machine gun to the roof of one of the unbombed hangars and was perched up there, popping away at the strafing planes.

Green men under fire acted like veterans. All moved swiftly to their places without any confusion or disorder. The cooks ran back into the kitchen to remove all the stored food to a safer place. The kitchen was hit. The staff sergeant in charge was struck on the head by a piece of shrapnel. He ripped off his shirt, tied up his head to stop the blood, and went on directing the work.

Outside, a corporal was speeding across the parade ground to help man a machine gun. The gun was entirely in the open, without any protection whatever. Halfway there the soldier was strafed by a low-flying Japanese pilot. Mortally wounded, he kept on, trying to get to the machine gun. He fell dead on the way.

His place was quickly taken. Eager privates ran out and took over the gun. They did this time and again, dashing out under fire and taking over free machine guns, even though the men who were operating them had just been strafed and killed. On the apron opposite the hangars a lone man was firing a .30 caliber machine gun which he had carried out and set up on the mount of a B-18 bomber. The gun was unstable, because the mount was made for an aerial gun. He braced it against his shoulder and kept up a steady stream of fire. An enemy plane flew low, strafed the plane he was in with incendiary bullets, and set it on fire. There was no way for the lone machine gunner to get out of his position in the nose of the bomber. Escape was impossible. All behind him was a flaming death trap. Spectators not far away said that he did not even try to get out, but kept on firing. Long after the leaping flames had enveloped the nose of the plane, they saw red tracer bullets from his machine gun mounting skyward.

There was humor with the tragedy. When the Japanese came over Hickam the third time, they placed a bomb squarely on the "Snake Ranch," the boys' name for their recently opened beer garden. A first sergeant of a truck company had endured the first two waves bravely enough, but this was too much. He dashed out of his barricade, shook his fist at the sky, and shouted, "You dirty S. O. B.'s! You've bombed the most important building on the Post!"

A group of U. S. bombers, all unarmed, were just

flying in from the mainland when the bewildered pilots suddenly found themselves pounced upon by a fleet of armed and shooting bombers.*Many of the Americans did not see the Rising Run on the planes and simply could not imagine what had broken loose above their heads. What kind of Hawaiian welcome was this?

A photographer in one of the American bombers assumed that the big ship approaching them had flown out to bid them *Aloha*. Happily, he mounted his high-speed camera at the window and "drew a bead" on the advancing bomber to make a picture record of the event. The Japanese, perhaps thinking the camera aimed directly at him was a gun, immediately swerved and withdrew from the area!

*See Chapter XIV: Historical Notes.

IV

AT PEARL HARBOR

ALL THAT HAPPENED AT THE AIRFIELDS WAS ONLY a prelude to the drama of Pearl Harbor. For years the Japanese have wanted to smash this Gibraltar of the Pacific. For years, its great three-fingered inlets have been the base from which the ships of Uncle Sam's Navy have operated on their annual Pacific maneuvers. If this modern harbor, extensive and complete enough to berth, repair, provision, and refit the entire United States fleet, could only be put out of commission, a powerful "threat to Japan's safety" would be pushed back two thousand miles across the ocean to California. "If we could only 'get' Pearl Harbor," the Japanese militarists told themselves, "we could raid the West Coast of the United States at will." And they could. Every detail of strategy in the attack showed that Pearl Harbor was the real objective. Planes were used in attacking it that never bothered to approach the landing fields. The attack lasted from 7:55 A.M. to 9:45 A.M.—a hundred and ten flaming minutes. There were one hundred and five Japanese planes—torpedo planes, strafers, dive bombers, and high-altitude horizontal bombers.*

Pearl Harbor is the United States' largest naval base, and its spacious waters can float every ship of any navy in the world. Battleships were there, those great warships named for the states in our union, anchored in the harbor. Destroyers lay near them, mine-layers, cruisers, and all the types of ships that the great navy of America boasts. There were eighty-six in all, and on each were boys and men of the United States Navy from virtually every city and county of the forty-eight states, from big cities and from small towns with such outlandish names as Wahoo, Nebraska, and Hominy, Oklahoma.*

A fearful surprise was in store for them, the most terrible in their lives, and the most astounding in the life of the U. S. Navy. From somewhere, exactly where they did not know, a wave of torpedo planes flying in from the direction of Honolulu—swift, low over the calm waters of the Harbor, eased down toward the ships, and released their torpedoes, glitter-

*See Chapter XIV: Historical Notes.

ing like fish in the sun, plunging with a loud splash into the sea.

You can tell a torpedo plane by the way it approaches its target. It comes down at an angle, levels off, and drops its torpedo as near the target as possible. The Japanese squadron of torpedo planes attacked in two waves. Each plane had its object carefully selected in advance, or so it seems, for the approaching ships separated and each went to a definite attack, the battleships getting it first.

From the crow's nest of one of the battleships, drawn up in a double two-mile lane in Battleship Row, a sailor saw one of the ugly mustard-colored planes heading toward the side of his ship.*He saw its deadly "fish," like a great shark, propellor for a tail, splash into the water below. The plane roared upward, barely clearing the deck of the ship. The sailor, paralyzed by the horrible fascination of awaiting the inevitable, watched the wake of the torpedo, coming straight for his ship. Massive battleship, of thousands of tons, it rocked as if hit by a mighty fist. Almost simultaneously with the horrendous roar which accompanied the blow, quantities of oil flew all over the ship. The oil caught on fire. In two minutes the deck of the ship, as long as a football field, was cov-

*See Chapter XIV: Historical Notes.

ered with flames, as if were an oil tanker that had
been hit. Flames leaped as high as the crow's nest on
which the lone sailor stood. Billows of heavy, oily
smoke enveloped him. It was like sticking his head in
a burning chimney flue to look over. Terrific heat,
smoke, the gas from the bomb blinded and choked
him. He fell to the floor of the crow's nest and hid
his face in his arms. Cries of the burned and wounded
below came up to him. He raised himself and tried to
look down. Cinders and flakes of burning paint flew
into his eyes and blinded him. Gropingly, he climbed
up on the edge of the crow's nest and leaped into the
oil-covered, flaming water below, just missing the
deck. He swam under water as long as he could, then
came up for breath. In a moment the burning oil
forced him under again. It was only a short way to
Ford Island, but when he clambered up on the beach,
every hair had been singed from his head. He gritted
his teeth, and joined a machine gun crew who were
already pouring lead into the Japanese planes.

In they came, flying down Battleship Row, as they
had flown down the rows of planes at Kaneohe,
Wheeler, Bellows, and Hickam. Here the targets were
bigger and easier to hit. As if they had rehearsed the
battle on a replica of Pearl Harbor set up somewhere
in Japan, twenty-one pilots of torpedo planes made

four attacks, supported by thirty dive bombers sweeping over twice during each onslaught. Simultaneously, from above, horizontal bombers pounded the decks of the eight battleships with high explosive bombs.

The torpedoes dropped by the first wave of planes wreaked the most havoc. They were specially designed for the attack on Pearl Harbor. They were not the ordinary type of air torpedoes at all, but a peculiarly deadly variation of the regular two-thousand pound torpedo carried by destroyers and submarines. The Japs had varied the recipe by putting in an extra load of TNT in the warhead as a substitute for the usual compressed air, which was not needed to propel the bombs the short distance they would need to go when released from the planes. The great grey warships were caught off guard, like sleeping giants struck by thunderbolts. *

Not a single battleship escaped one or more staggering body blows. The sound of explosions, followed by the din and clangor of steel twisted and rent, tore the air. The *Arizona, Oklahoma, California,* and *West Virginia* sank to the shallow, muddy bottom of the harbor in a matter of minutes after they were struck.

The enemy planes whizzed deafeningly over each American ship for a second, dropping their bombs and strafing the seamen on the decks. One ship was

*See Chapter XIV: Historical Notes.

turning over. Smoke belched out from others. On decks, anti-aircraft guns wheeled skyward, pounded and roared. Stretcher teams, amid a hail of machine gun bullets, ran swiftly to retrieve the wounded. Battle commands were roared through the loud speaker systems. Seamen manned their battle stations.

Below decks, heavy sea water rushed into gaping holes blown in the sides of battleships. Men were trapped, some by the water, some in compartments which sealed them in as massive steel doors automatically closed to prevent the water from rushing into further sections of the ship.

Above decks, men who had stuck to their ships until the final moments when remaining aboard was useless, now leapt into the water, struck out for other ships, climbed aboard and fought on from there. The comparative safety of the shore lay only a few yards away, but getting back into battle took precedence over saving their own lives.

As it became evident that it was impossible for certain ships to stay afloat, medical personnel carried ashore their dressings, splints, and medicated liquid to treat burns, and continued their work on the docks —under heavy gun fire. As wounded men weighed down with heavy fuel oil dragged themselves out of the burning waters, they found first aid stations set up on the beach and at various landings to relieve their suffering.

Gigs, tugboats, and motor launches sped across Pearl Harbor's reverberating channel. One Naval Reserve ensign and a crew of four volunteers had already saved nearly a hundred men who had been injured or blown overboard into the oil-fired waters. Suddenly, in close proximity to a burning battleship, the launch's propeller jammed. Calmly, the ensign directed the work of disengaging the screw as flames licked the small boat's hull. Simultaneously, he continued supervising the picking up of more victims from the harbor.

Under continuous gun fire and raining shrapnel, coxwains made repeated trips from ship to shore, rescuing men hurled overboard, picking up some of the thousands who were jumping from the decks and portholes of sinking or burning ships. As "bow hook" of a gig, Seaman Joseph Bednorz pulled man after man from the flaming waters. Some of the wounded were taken aboard the hospital ship *Solace* for treatment. Captain William H. Michael saw scores of wounded men landed where the *USS Argonne*, flagship of the Base Force, was docked. The rescuers urgently needed stretchers to replace those on which the wounded men were transferred to the dock. Carpenters, sailmakers, and shipfitters on the *Argonne* quickly knocked together stout canvas and wood carriers, and the rescue crews turned back to the work of searching the waters for the wounded.

At Ford Island, the Naval Air Station in Pearl Harbor, the enlisted men's quarters were ablaze, and hangars were on fire, smoke pouring through dark holes in the glass wall fronts. Before the burning hangars, a short distance from the water, smoked the charred remains of three or four squadrons of what had been proud patrol bombers—Catalinas or PBYs.

Antonia Di Napoli, whose home address is "Wild Cat Canyon, California," and Roy Bratton fought blazing fires which threatened to destroy three planes, drawing water from the harbor itself.

The runway, backbone of the two-mile island was strewn with bomb fragments, Japanese machine gun bullets flattened and misshapen by the concrete, and empty cartridges that had fallen from the attacking planes.

The mighty radio antenna serving the air station was shot down. To assist in restoring it, Arthur Balfour, at the height of the attack, climbed to the top of the building on which the wires had fallen. He was in direct line of the enemy strafing attacks and our own defensive fire, but neither Japanese nor American bullets whizzing past drove him from his perch. As Balfour worked, Radioman McCormick climbed even higher into the danger zone. He scaled an unprotected smokestack, a slim finger reaching into the sky. There he clung, shells bursting all around him, until he had restored the antenna.

A yeoman, seaman second-class, was filing liberty cards on the second deck inside the *Oklahoma* when the call came, in a calm tone, "Unengaged personnel lay to third deck!"

As he went down the ladder, the same officer's voice yelled to him through the loud speaker system, "All hands to General Quarters! This is no s . . . ! The Japs are attacking!"

The yeoman felt the ship jar and shake. He ran aft to the next compartment. The ship was listing. As he came out on deck by his battle station, holding on to the galley ladder to keep from slipping, he heard a man crying out. He turned and saw a seaman caught by a heavy door which had closed when the ship listed. The yeoman started to help, but as he let go his hold on the galley door, he slid down the crazily tipping deck. He landed in three feet of water which had already risen to the deck as the ship turned over.

He made his way back to the door and helped the

struggling seaman release himself. Both then began
to pull themselves upward on the increasingly steep
deck. Seamen by the hundreds were attempting to
cling to the deck. The yeoman saw the chief commis-
sary steward fall half a dozen times. All hands strained
upward toward the "lifeline"—three chains strung as
railings on the battleship. If they could make the lifeline, they could then slide down the hull of the capsizing ship and land in the water only a few feet from
Ford Island. Otherwise, they would have to swim
completely around the sinking ship—a perilously long
journey in the flaming waters. The men reached the
welcome chain, pulled themselves to it, and slid down
the side to safety.

A chaplain was below in his cabin when the first
explosion came. He leaped to the porthole. The level
of the water, ordinarily eight or nine feet below the
opening, was only six inches from his face, and covered with oil. At the moment he looked out, the ship
was hit again. Water gushed into the cabin. He turned
the catch to lock the porthole just in time. As he did,
the ship listed farther, and through the glass he saw
the water completely submerge the porthole. He
turned to the door and heard the rush of water down
the passageway. When he opened it, the torrent of
water surged into his room. By the time he had fought

his way to the top of the ladder, the whole compartment below him was filled with oil and water.

As the chaplain stepped out on deck, a bomber flying almost directly above him dropped an incendiary bomb. Instantly, hundreds of squares of red-hot steel were flying at him, and all over the ship. A fire sprang up wherever one of the red squares came to rest. The chaplain leaped behind the combing of the hatch and escaped being injured.

In the next second a bomb landed, knocking one of the ship's airplanes from its catapult. As it crashed to the deck, a pontoon broke off and came hurtling toward the chaplain. It hit the hatch-combing behind which he crouched, and flew off into the water. It would have been death to move. To walk out now was to enter a wall of shrapnel and machine gun fire.

This hell lasted until the first wave of airplanes withdrew—perhaps twenty minutes. Suddenly the clamor ceased, and the chaplain could hear voices on the nearby shore of Ford Island. The *Oklahoma* was listing badly. The order came to abandon ship. Behind the hatch, on the side of the ship away from Ford Island, a young ensign and two enlisted men were struggling to release a life raft. It had been caught in the deck rigging, and they could not approach it from their side. The chaplain stepped up to it and, with the super-strength that comes in such moments, shoved it out. From the raft, the chaplain, the ensign, and the two men rescued others who had left the ship and were struggling in the oily water. Many of them were so completely covered with the heavy fuel oil that they could not open their eyes. Several were vomiting, sick from swallowing oil and salt water. While they labored at their rescue work, a Japanese plane, one of the second wave, swooped down and strafed them, but missed. The rescuers collected twenty-eight men and took them ashore to the Navy Yard, opposite Ford Island.

Hundreds were still on the ship. Among them was a young lieutenant, lying dazed on the deck. He and his men had been dogging down the hatches when the first torpedo hit, rocking them like peanuts in a bag. Fumes from the fuel oil mixed with ether from the medical supply room, which had been hit, over- whelmed them. Not knowing what was choking them, they ran to the forward compartment for gas masks. When they opened the door of this compartment, they found twelve or fifteen helpless men, some stand- ing knee-deep in oily water, some fainting and falling. The lieutenant and his men dragged the sufferers into the next compartment, but the passage through which they had to go belched such a quantity of fumes that the whole crowd were overcome, falling to the floor unconscious.

The young lieutenant came to on deck. He had been pulled out and taken aft. As he awoke, a bomb hit the compartment they had just left. It was the most terrific explosion that had yet occurred. The concussion caused by thousands of pounds of TNT sent every loose thing on the ship flying. Paint was jarred loose from every part of the ship's deck and flew off as if hit by a thousand invisible chip hammers. The lieutenant's hair was filled with it. The heat ignited the fresh paint on a turret, which burst into flames. A lad was climbing an outside ladder. The concussion blew him into the iron rungs. His body came through on the other side in as many pieces as the sections he covered. One seaman was blown against a bulkhead. Identification was impossible.

The young lieutenant was rescued.

The members of a turret crew were trying frantically to find their way out of their pitchblack prison. James Ward, a twenty-year-old seaman first class, found a flashlight and trained it on the compartment door. It was already late, the *Oklahoma* was sinking fast, yet the young seaman remained in the turret holding the flashlight so the rest of the crew could escape. He was awarded posthumous honors.

Down inside the overturning ship a young chaplain was working swiftly and silently by a porthole, helping other men to get through. His turn to leave had come many times, but he stayed on until the last man in line was helped out. Then it was too late for the chaplain to escape. "Go ahead, boys. I'm all right!" were his last words.

Men sacrificed their blood and life's breath in order to keep up their part of the fight even for a few minutes longer. An ensign, Herbert Charpiot Jones, manned a three-inch battery on the *California* until the mechanical ammunition hoists were put out of action. Any place on a burning ship is dangerous, but the ammunition supply room is the most dangerous of all. Nevertheless, Ensign Jones organized a party of volunteers to go below. There they worked, no words passing between them, in constant danger of being blown to bits. They carried ammunition through flaming compartments, supplying other batteries with shells with which to fight off the Japanese. A bomb exploded, and the shrapnel flying from it mortally wounded the brave ensign. His men attempted to carry him away from the area, which was on fire, but he ordered them to abandon him. "Leave me alone, I am done for!" he commanded. "Get out of here before the magazines go off!" He died by his post.

Thomas J. Reeves, chief radioman, took up a post in a burning passageway and passed ammunition by hand to the anti-aircraft gunners. The smoke choked him and fire burned him. Others left, but something in Reeves made him stay on, serving the battery until he was fatally overcome by the smoke and fire.

So it was, too, with Ensign Robert R. Scott, machinist's mate. With others, he was in the *California's* air compressor compartment, keeping up air for the guns above. A tremendous explosion knocked them all to the floor. A torpedo had hit the ship. Water rushed into their compartment and was rising in a flood. The order came to evacuate, and all the rest of the group obeyed except Ensign Scott. The last words that anyone heard him speak were, "This is my station, and by God, I will stay and give them air as long as the guns are going!"

The *Utah*, anchored midway in Battleship Row, received a terrific pounding from the air as well as from torpedoes below.[*] It soon became cruelly evident that she was rapidly capsizing. "Abandon ship!" the

*See Chapter XIV: Historical Notes.

cry came from Lieutenant Commander Isquith, and the men leapt overboard like schools of fish. With them went Coxswain Bruner, who recovered his motor launch, which had been set adrift by the parting of the boat's lines. Aided by one man, Bruner miraculously escaped enemy strafing and bombing while he rescued his shipmates from the water about the sinking ship.

Signalman Joseph Vonhosser had no rescue boat, but he reached out to a floundering mate and helped him to shore. Then Vonhosser dived back into the water and, acting as a one-man rescue party, swam to the *Utah*'s side four more times, assisting shipmates in distress to safety on each trip.

Ninety per cent of the crew escaped. Among the ten per cent who did not was Peter Tomich, chief water tender. Although he heard the call to abandon ship and realized that his ship was capsizing, Tomich remained steadfastly at his post in the engineering plant. He refused to leave until he made sure that all boilers were secured and that all other men in the fireroom had escaped to safety. By that time, it was too late for him to leave his station and to save his own life. *

The *Nevada* had steam up and was making a dash to sea. The Japs were bombing her without mercy,

*See Chapter XIV: Historical Notes.

hoping to sink her in the channel. Her twenty-nine thousand tons of steel would choke the entrance and bottle up the fleet. All her anti-aircraft guns were spitting fire and lead. There was an explosion so tremendous that even amid the terrific roar of battle the men on other ships looked up from their guns. Two high explosive bombs had landed almost simultaneously on the *Nevada's* deck. Many of the thirteen hundred men on the ship were blown overboard, some killed, others wounded. The decks were littered with the injured. Yet only one anti-aircraft gun stopped firing. This was the gun of which Marine Corporal J. R. Driscoll was captain. His gun was completely demolished, the crew killed. Driscoll was wounded, and most of his clothes were burned off his body, but he ran to help man another gun whose crew had suffered casualties.

Ensign J. K. Taussig, Jr., senior officer of another battery, received serious wounds from flying shrapnel. His men tried to make him lie down, but he refused to leave his battle station. It took another hero, Pharmicist's Mate Ned Curtis, to save him. Not waiting for a lull in the attack, Curtis climbed the foremast structure to the anti-aircraft director while the enemy planes zoomed low overhead, bombing and strafing. Disregarding Ensign Taussig's order to go below, Curtis, himself severely burned, placed the wounded officer on a stretcher. Other means of descent blocked by fire caused by a bomb explosion, Curtis enlisted the aid of others and lowered Ensign Taussig three deck levels to the boat deck.

The *Nevada* had more than her share of heroes. G. D. Etcell, chief shipfitter, was in charge of fire, flood, and damage control. He was headed forward to determine whether a magazine group had been flooded. Without a moment's hesitation he risked his life, plunging into acrid smoke and through hot water up to his waist in order to obtain the information. In the magazine room he came upon a shipmate, unconscious from the smoke and fumes. Etcell carried the man to safety.

Heat in the forward dynamo was becoming humanly unbearable. Machinist D. K. Ross forced his men to leave, but he remained and performed all their duties himself. Finally, blinded and unconscious, he fell out into the passageway. When he recovered, Ross returned and secured his own station, then proceeded to the after dynamo room where he was again overcome by fumes and intense heat. For a third time he doggedly fought his way back to consciousness and returned to his battle station where he remained until ordered to abandon it.

Ensign Thomas H. Saylor assumed control of the

port anti-aircraft battery. A bomb exploded nearby. Shell fragments from it sank into his flesh, its heat set his clothes on fire and burned him, the concussion broke both his eardrums. Yet he stuck to his guns and even had the presence of mind to notice that some "ready-boxes" of ammunition nearby were becoming heated. Entirely disregarding his own condition, he immediately played a stream of water on them and prevented casualties and heavy damage to the battery.

The *Nevada* cleared the channel, and her Captain grounded her at Hospital Point. Now, no matter how much the Japs pummeled her, they could not sink her. Furthermore, she was in a convenient position where she could be quickly repaired.*

The *West Virginia* was sinking and taking a severe beating while she went down. As Captain Mervyn Bennion emerged from the conning tower to the bridge, the better to direct the fight, fragments from a bursting bomb hit him and laid his stomach completely open. He tried to stand, but could not, and fell to the deck from where he continued to direct the defense of the ship. Two officers and a Negro mess attendant carried the captain away from the flames but he refused all attempts to remove him from the bridge.* When the bridge became a blazing inferno,

*See Chapter XIV: Historical Notes.

the officers and messman tried again to carry Captain Bennion to safety, but he ordered them away. "Save yourselves!" he commanded. Even as he uttered the words, the leaping flames enveloped his body.*

The Negro mess attendant, Dorie Miller, had raced up from the galley when the first load of bombs burst on the *West Virginia*. Now, while the universe itself seemed to be exploding, Miller manned a machine gun. He had never fired such a weapon before, but now he fought beside the trained officers until all of their guns were rendered useless by fires started by the bombs falling around them. When they attempted to go below, they saw that fire had blocked all usual means of retreat from the bridge. After almost unbearable punishment from the heat, the three fighters were thrown a line from a boat crane. Progressing hand over hand along the cable, they made their way to safety.

Two eighteen-year-old lads were ironing out their uniforms in the press room of the *USS Tennessee* when a voice sounded over one of the loud speakers, calling, "All men man stations! All men man stations!"

"It looks like we're going to have a 'dry run'," Marine Private Coy Tyson said. "Come along and I'll show you a big gun."

*See Chapter XIV: Historical Notes.

His friend, Private Harry Polto of the U. S. Army, was visiting that Sunday on a battleship for the first time in his life. They hit the deck and ran to Tyson's battle station.

Then it seemed to the boys that everything happened at once. As they looked out over the harbor, they saw a big explosion on another battleship not far away. Then came a series of sharp cracks like a whole carload of firecrackers going off at once.

Polto looked up into the sky. He saw a flight of planes, smoke pouring out of their machine guns. He looked down at his feet. Splinters of wood spurted up from the deck. He and Tyson dove for the protection of a nearby gun turret. They watched the Jap planes drop their bombs. Some hit their targets, others exploded in the water. One bomb struck a turret on the *Tennessee*, but did little damage.

"Machine gun volunteers!" came the call from one of the marine captains.

"Let's go!" yelled Polto. He knew a little about the operation of a machine gun. The captain put them to work, Tyson feeding the ammunition while Polto fired a .30 calibre Lewis gun.

A Jap plane flew low overhead. It fired away with a burst of bullets that hit not a yard away from the two boys. They tried hard to shoot it down, but failed.

Another enemy plane came in from a distance and swooped down low to machine gun sailors and marines who had abandoned ship and were swimming for the shore. Then it headed for a destroyer directly in its path, a destroyer so near the *Tennessee* that the Jap plane was in easy target range of the two young machine gunners. The plane dropped a bomb which missed the destroyer and plunged into the water. As the plane pulled up from its dive, Private Polto caught the Japanese pilot squarely in the sights of his machine gun and blazed away. Others were doubtless shooting at him, too, but there was no quarrel as to who got him. The important thing was that the plane went out of control and crashed in the waters of Pearl Harbor.

When Polto returned to Schofield Barracks the next afternoon, he carried with him an unusual document for a soldier to possess—a commendation for valor under fire aboard a United States battleship, signed by the executive officer of the *USS Tennessee*.

Possibly the most terrific series of explosions that the peaceful island of Oahu has known since the eruption centuries ago of the extinct volcanic craters of Punchbowl and Diamond Head occurred on the *Arizona*. Earlier in the attack a torpedo had hit the battleship. Now a flight of horizontal bombers, flying high above their own torpedo planes and air bombers, at an altitude of ten thousand feet, dropped a series of armor-piercing bombs almost simultaneously on the stationary vessel below. Their immense weight drove them through several decks before they exploded. One dropped like a plummet straight down the funnel and blew up the ship's forward magazine where ammunition was stored.* Torpedoes and high-powered explosives joined the bombs. The inside of the whole forward ship blew up instantly. The after part of the ship shook as if it would fall apart like a stack of cards. The forecastle waved up and down. Turrets jumped into the air and came down again. Fire and smoke pushed up through the seams of the deck.

A great swishing sound, followed by a tremendous boom, accompanied the explosion. It was a strange sound to all ears, but every one of the thousands on the other ships and on shore knew what it meant . . .

Human beings on the ship were helpless. Bodies flew two and three hundred feet into the air, hurled about as tiny particles are whisked aloft in an uncontrollable fire.

Rear Admiral Isaac C. Kidd, whose flag flew from the *Arizona's* mast, was on the ship. He had fought her

---

*See Chapter XIV: Historical Notes.

until now, but when the magazine exploded he met death on the bridge. Captain Franklin Van Valkenburg, commander of the battleship, also died at his post, trying until the last to hold himself erect against the rail.

The members of the *Arizona's* band manned their battle stations immediately. Their post was on a lower deck, far below the water line; their job—passing ammunition. All twenty-one of the ship's musicians had graduated together from the School of Music at the Washington Navy Yard the previous May. Now all twenty-one of them died together when the *Arizona's* magazine exploded.

A group of twenty men and officers were trapped in Turret III. All lights went out. A hot blast enveloped them in the darkness. They felt pressure on their ear drums. Nauseating gas and smoke smothered them. All communication with the outside was gone—ship's service phones, battle phones, and high power phones were cut off.

"What kind of gas is it?" a seaman asked, choking.

"Yes, what kind is it?" others asked excitedly.

There was confusion and danger of panic, but at one command, "Quiet!" not a word was spoken.

"Breathe through your clothes," Lieutenant Jim Dick Miller directed.

A seaman produced a flashlight, and with it they found their way through the thick smoke to the ladder. The man sent up to open the hatch took a long time. The others waited in the heavy smoke. Coughing became louder and louder. No one cried out, "For God's sake, hurry!" They waited like professional seamen. The hatch was finally opened and they got out.

They burst out upon an amazing sight. The forward part of the ship was a mass of shattered, burning wood and twisted metal. Bodies of the dead were thick on the deck, and some were hanging from the forecastle. Men were running out of the flames, falling on the deck, jumping over the side. Japanese planes were flying low over the ship, strafing the fleeing seamen and those huddled together under the turrets. A Marine lieutenant lay on his back with blood on his shirt front. A corporal running by bent over him, took him by the shoulders, and asked if there was anything he could do. The young lieutenant was too near death to answer.

Out of the chaos the men heard a voice of calm reassurance.

"Take it easy. Don't get excited. Leave the ship for Ford Island." They followed the instructions.

It was the voice of the ranking surviving officer,

Lieutenant Commander Samuel Fuqua, supervising the saving of the wounded. He went into the flames. Many who came walking out with him were so badly burned that they were barely able to stand. Clothes burned away, no eyelashes, no hair, they stumbled along, feeling their way, helpless, yet not a man of them uttering a groan or a cry.

One boy about twenty-one, with wide blue eyes, kept repeating, "I can't see. I can't see." The officer passed his hands in front of his staring eyes. They did not flicker.

Commander Fuqua worked swiftly, surely, and took no shelter the whole time, coming out of the flames into machine gun fire sent down by the Japanese, who continued to strafe the wounded and dying. Wooden splinters flew around him from the deck, spattered by the bullets. Many of the wounded and some of those unhurt would have failed to get off the burning ship had it not been for the commander's presence of mind and his unmatchable courage. Men took heart from his calmness, forgot about themselves, and turned to fight the fire or help others escape.*

"When are you leaving, sir?" someone asked.

"Not until the Japs leave!" he answered through the flames.

*See Chapter XIV: Historical Notes.

Eventually he gave the order to abandon ship, and the cry was taken up by all hands.

"Abandon ship! Abandon ship!"

Before they left, six or seven men opened all the hatches. One man below breathed the air of freedom again.

Many of the men in quitting the ship leaped overboard, leaving their room in the boat for the wounded. The oil was so thick on the surface that they could hardly swim. A marine major, struggling toward shore, saw a man who was going under. The major was very tired, knew they both would probably drown, but he grabbed the fellow's shirt and said, "Hold on to my shoulder!" A few yards farther on, the major floundered. The other loosened his grip.

"Make it alone, Major!"

The major grabbed the panting man by his shirt and held him up, refusing to let go until they both reached the beach.

The last thing the boys in the small boat saw as they pulled away with the final load of wounded was Commander Fuqua, alone on the quarterdeck, the ship aflame from Turret III forward. When he had made sure that no one else was left alive on the ship, he leaped overboard and swam ashore.

Meanwhile the *Vestal*, a repair ship drawn up alongside the *Arizona*, was seeing action. Commander Cassin Young, realizing that the gunnery officer was not on board, manned the ship's sole 3-inch anti-aircraft gun himself, permitting no one else to touch it while he blazed away at incoming Jap planes. *

Two big explosive bombs struck the vessel and knocked the Commander down. He jumped up, grabbed the gun again and resumed shooting. At this moment occurred the explosion of the *Arizona's* forward magazine. The concussion blew the plucky little Commander across the lifeline and into the sea.

"Abandon ship!" ordered the executive officer left on board.

The men were going down the gangplank when their skipper bobbed up out of the water.

"Hey, where you fellows going!" he demanded.

They told him that, under orders, they were abandoning ship.

"The hell you are!" he shouted. "Get back to your stations!"

As the men returned to their posts, the skipper scurried aboard and again took up his position at the gun. Wringing wet, amid the severe enemy bombing and strafing, he shouted some of the smartest orders of the day. In fifteen minutes his men got the *Vestal*

*See Chapter XIV: Historical Notes.

underway, cleared the *Arizona*, and saved their ship by beaching her.*

On the white hospital ship *Solace*, also anchored near the *Arizona*, the blast from the big battleship blew the clothes off several of the men on deck. The terrific heat from the huge neighbor ship, blanketed with smoke, burning fiercely—throwing flames one hundred feet high, threatened to set off boxes of ammunition on the deck of the *Solace*. Disregarding their fate had the shells exploded, members of the gun crew lay themselves down on the cases, shielding the ammunition from the heat with their own bodies as the ship pulled out past the flaming *Arizona*.*

As the *Solace* moved through the thick layer of burning fuel oil about the sinking ship, it passed men swimming desperately, trying to save themselves. One officer, choking, and weakened from struggling in the heavy oil, went under. Frederic Ley, Fireman second class, saw him. He leapt overboard into the flaming oil, and rescued the drowning man. Boats were lowered and crewmen and hospital corpsmen dragged other victims out of the oil and took them on board the Solace and to the landings about Pearl Harbor.

*See Chapter XIV: Historical Notes.

On one ship something went wrong with the power hoist.* "Pass the ammunition by hand!" the order came, and it was no small order considering the speed with which the five-inch anti-aircraft guns had to be fed. Almost at once, lines of men formed, stretching endlessly from each stuttering gun into the ammunition chambers far below decks, passing shell after shell to the ever-empty maw of the anti-aircraft. No time to rest or wipe away their sweat, they kept passing to the gunners, who loaded and fired, reloaded and fired again.

Through the scorching haze enveloping the powder-grimed men of the ammunition line went Chaplain Howell Forgy, a striking figure, walking up and down, talking to this man, giving that one a pat on the back, wiping the sweat from another's face. He would have liked to be in there fighting, but international law forbade him from battle action and restricted him only to encouraging the living, and comforting the wounded and dying.

"Hey Padre! You gonna hold service?" yelled one husky lad from the line.

The Chaplain looked the seaman in the eye and said, "Praise the Lord—*and pass the ammunition!*"

From then on, every time a shell hit the breech of

*See Chapter XIV: Historical Notes.

the anti-aircraft gun, someone shouted "Hallelujah! Praise the Lord and pass the ammunition! Hallelujah!"

By one of the many coincidences attending the attack, eighteen scout bombing planes from a U. S. aircraft carrier flew into the fight at Pearl Harbor before they knew it.* They were set upon by numerically superior forces and four were shot down.

One of these was piloted by Flight Lieutenant Clarence Dickinson. Lt. Dickinson's gunner was killed, and his plane shot out of control in the air above Barber's Point, some twenty miles from Pearl Harbor. Fire forced the Lieutenant to bail out. He made his way to the Naval Air Base, and without even mentioning his recent harrowing experience to the commanding officer, he immediately took off in another plane, and set out on a hundred and seventy-five mile search flight.

As Ensign E. T. Deacon, of scouting squadron 6, returned his plane to Pearl Harbor, heavy smoke and groups of Japanese planes warned him away and he attempted to land at Luke Field, instead. There, attacked by enemy Zero fighters, he headed for Hickam Field, but lost power when his engine was hit. He stalled into the water just short of the Army Air Base. Both he and his radioman were wounded.

*See Chapter XIV: Historical Notes.

Deacon bandaged his crewman's arm, broke out the lifecraft, and paddled to shore to safety.

Thirty-seven other Navy planes were able to reach the air. Two were JRS amphibian planes, not equipped with any armament. Contact with an enemy plane would mean almost certain death in these unprotected ships. Yet there was no lack of volunteers for the mission to discover desperately needed information of the enemy's movements.

One plane was shot from under aviation radioman Oscar Benefiel as he prepared it to leave the field, yet he immediately went up as crew member in another plane. They were equipped only with Springfield rifles with which possibly to face .50 caliber Japanese machine guns, yet Benefiel and four others showed no hesitation as, rifles across their laps, their plane left the field.

Some of the scout planes were attacked. Robert Baxter, radio gunner in one, carried on a running battle with a modern Japanese fighting plane. Baxter handled his machine gun so well that the enemy plane was forced to break off the engagement and withdraw, smoke trailing behind him.

Perhaps the most gruelling experience of the day among the Navy searchers was that of William Russell Roberts, Aviation Radioman First Class. As radioman-gunner of a battleship scout plane, he remained out on his search mission until about ten o'clock that night. When his pilot, Lieutenant J. B. Ginn, tried to land on the blacked out island, the plane crashed in heavy seas about eight miles offshore at Barbers Point. Roberts received a severe cut in the head and fell unconscious. When he came to, he freed himself from his parachute and the cockpit, reached the surface of the water, and inflated his lifejacket. He dived for the pilot, but the heavy seas were shifting the plane in the dark, so he had difficulty in finding him. Finally he located Ginn, unconscious, his right leg jammed between the seat and the fuselage. Roberts succeeded in freeing him, inflated his life jacket, and placed him on a wing float so he could breathe. By repeated diving, despite cuts and bruises, once almost drowning when he became entangled, Roberts freed the rubber life boat from the plane. He succeeded in shoving the unconscious pilot to the rubber raft and struck out for shore.

When they reached the heavy surf which beats the sand at this point, a large breaker capsized the boat, and Lieutenant Ginn, still unconscious, rolled back into the ocean. Roberts searched in the blackness until he found the pilot, dragged him ashore, gave him first aid and hiked for help. He did not find

it until one o'clock that morning. An Army patrol
took them both to the hospital, where it required
fifteen stitches to close the wounds in Roberts' head.
Despite the young radioman's heroic attempt to save
his pilot, Lieutenant Ginn did not survive the ordeal.

The *Arizona* was lost, and a thousand men with
her. The *Oklahoma* had turned over, men inside
clamoring to get out. The *California* and the *West
Virginia* had settled in the mud of the Harbor, with
only their turrets projecting above the water. The
Nevada was beached, and the old decommissioned
target ship *Utah* sunk, lying on her side on the bottom
of the harbor. The destroyers *Cassin* and *Downes*
seemed completely wrecked, blown to bits; the
destroyer *Shaw* and a large floating dry dock nearby
were so severely damaged that repair seemed hopeless. The minelayer *Oglala* was done for. Smoke was
pouring out of the *Maryland*, the *Tennessee*, and the
Pennsylvania. The *Helena, Honolulu,* and *Raleigh,*
—three cruisers that were among the first to put up
an anti-aircraft barrage—were damaged, along with
the seaplane tender *Curtis* and the repair ship *Vestal*.
Men were killed and wounded, dying on every
air field, in Pearl Harbor, and in the streets of Honolulu. Airplanes, ships, and homes were afire, but the

Japanese imperialists lit a new fire that day which, praise be to the allied armies, will sweep over the world, carrying democracy and liberation even to Japan's own people.

Even that day, the attackers got a taste of what is to come. Once the first shock had passed, America swerved and hit back. From every part of the island, defense forces rose to action.

They were led by a seaman first class who was writing a letter near one of the machine gun nests on his "battlewagon" when the first of a line of enemy planes came over. Recognizing the insignia on the wings, he manned a machine gun, fired at the planes following, scoring several hits. He downed his first plane before "General Quarters"—the call to battle stations—rang out.

In four minutes after the first alarm, which sounded just before eight A.M., the fleet's guns went into action. Batteries from the largest rapid fire anti-aircraft guns down to Lewis machine guns, automatic rifles, and pistols, sent up a formidable, lethal umbrella barrage. With each passing minute, Pearl Harbor became a more perilous death trap for Japanese airmen. One bomber which crashed and burned in the Naval Hospital grounds during the second attack about nine

A.M. was struck by shells and machine gun bullets from as many as fourteen different ships. In spite of the admitted success of their surprise, the Japanese paid a high price for it in the loss of torpedo, dive bombing, and horizontal bombing planes shot down by converging fire of the fleet ships. In the first half-hour, the American seamen fighters picked off Jap planes at the rate of one every three minutes. Army and Navy men together brought down forty-eight of the estimated one hundred and five attacking planes. This is a good shooting average even under the most favorable conditions.

Men fought with the cool confidence that comes from complete indoctrination for battle. In one case a single bluejacket manned a five-inch anti-aircraft gun after his ten battery mates had been shot down in a strafing attack. The lone sailor seized the heavy shells from the fuse-pot, placed them in the tray, dashed to the other side of the gun, and rammed the shells home. Then he leapt to position on the pointer's seat and fired. Loading, ramming, firing, he kept up the work of eleven men until a terrific explosion blew him over the side of his battleship. He was rescued.

The Destroyer *Shaw* was in a marine railway at the time of the attack, but, fully manned and armed, it began pouring lead into the attacking planes. She

AT PEARL HARBOR   103

was hit repeatedly by bombs, but kept on firing, and brought down more than one enemy plane. Then the Japanese concentrated on the plucky destroyer for a prolonged attack, plane after plane diving in, pounding her decks with demolition and high explosive bombs. Finally, one bomb reached the *Shaw's* magazine. A huge ball of red fire erupted from her, shooting like a rocket five hundred feet into the air. Only then did her crew cease firing.

Civilian workers fighting fire at the floating dry dock rushed to the aid of the damaged *Shaw*. One fireman, Iver Carlson, was working near the service ammunition when it exploded from the heat. The sharp sting of shrapnel told him he was wounded in the face and right arm. Yet he kept the hose trained on the fire and refused to leave the ship until compelled to by a commissioned officer.

In the wardroom of the fifteen hundred ton destroyer, *Allwyn*, Ensign S. Caplan and three reserve ensigns heard the announcement from the bridge telephone: "The *Utah* has been torpedoed by Japanese aircraft!"

Immediately they sounded General Quarters and manned their battle stations. As senior officer, Ensign Caplan gave orders to get under way at once. One of the reserve officers took the bridge with the senior officer, another took the guns, and the third became damage-control officer.

Five minutes later they opened against the enemy with their machine guns. Japanese planes were diving at ships in the harbor. Two minutes later Ensign Caplan brought his large caliber anti-aircraft battery into action.

Below decks, the chief machinist's mate, acting as engineering officer, lit off another boiler. Fortunately, they already had steam under one. The chief boatswain's mate led his repair party into the job of clearing ship for action.

Within a short time they were heading for the channel. A gun jammed. The chief gunner's mate ordered all his men away from the gun shield and out of the handling room. At the risk of being blown to bits, he cleared the jammed shell, called the men back, and continued firing.

As they moved downstream, they kept up a hot fire with their main battery and machine guns. Four planes were shot, smoking, from the sky. Two planes roared over the destroyer, trying to reach the battleships beyond. Machine guns brought them down.

Abeam Fort Weaver, Ensign Caplan called for more knots. The chief gave them. They sped out of the harbor, heading for their area.

The chief radioman got a good contact on his listening apparatus.

"Submarine!"

They maneuvered the destroyer for the attack and dropped two depth charges. Then they regained contact and dropped two more.

A large oil slick appeared on the sea and bubbles covered the surface for two hundred feet. They had sunk their first sub.

Suddenly another contact was reported. The destroyer made an emergency turn and attacked. From the racks the ensigns loosed another pair of depth charges. When they swung around again they saw another oil slick. They had sunk a second submarine.

From then on they screened the cruiser. Though the *Allwyn* had expended hundreds of rounds of high-explosive shells and thousands of rounds of machine gun bullets, the destroyer's young officers returned her to Pearl Harbor when the battle was over, without a single casualty.*

On every ship men leaped to their battle stations and poured out reprisal fire from anti-aircraft and machine guns. When the *Oklahoma* began to turn over, its fighting crew followed it around as it capsized, firing their guns until they went under water.

*See Chapter XIV: Historical Notes.

They swam to the dock, cheering a more fortunate ship than their own as it cleared the harbor.

Several men under treatment in the hospital ship *Solace* leapt from their beds, in spite of protests and attempted restraint by medical officers and nurses. They left the ship in a small boat and joined up with fighting units repelling the attack from other ships.

All guns were put into use. A country lad from the west, a lowly "boot-seaman," had a standard rifle shoved in his hand.

"Get out and shoot!" was the command.

A small dive bomber came in, poised to drop a bomb. The boy had not been trained to handle a heavy rifle, but he had "done lots of huntin'" in his day. He took a bead and fired. One of the freak accidents of the war occurred. Apparently the boys' bullet hit the detonator of the bomb the Japanese was about to drop, for the plane simply burst in mid-air and disintegrated before their eyes. The boy fainted on the deck.

Officers and men everywhere worked together and set each other inspiring examples. A first lieutenant of one ship exposed himself continuously to the enemy strafing while directing operations on the quarter-deck and boatdeck. He ordered men not engaged to keep back in sheltered areas, but he himself remained constantly exposed in order to direct the work of damage control and putting out fires.

His example was followed by the boatswain's mate, who was sent to the booth of the officer of the deck to phone the central engine room to put more pressure on the fire mains. While he was phoning, a bomb struck near the booth and enveloped him in flames. He stayed at the telephone to get the message through.

A chief gunner was lying in his bunk recovering from yellow fever shots. The first torpedo hit just forward below him. He was thrown to the ceiling, and landed with a wrenched back. Fuel oil was coming in. Forgetting his back, he ran to the magazine to help get anti-aircraft ammunition going up to his battle station. Men there were being overcome by fumes from the fuel oil, and were falling on the deck. A man sent to the phone to call for help was enveloped in the fumes and fell to the deck. The gunner took the telephone and called the Sky Control.

"Men for the five-inch anti-aircraft!" he shouted.

He turned to the guns, but there was no more ammunition. He dashed back to the ammunition room. The floor was strewn with asphyxiated men. He started getting out ammunition himself, and fell to the floor in a faint.

The gunner woke that afternoon on a mess table in the marine grounds, his back hurting. He was naked. Rescuers had removed his oil-soaked clothes. He leaped from the table; ran to the supply room, got a shirt, shoes, and trousers, and headed back for his battle station. He was stopped and sent to hospital.

Two marines were manning a machine gun. A Japanese plane flew low and dropped a bomb which exploded on the deck. A burning fragment sank into the back of the marine firing. While his mate tugged at the jagged steel and pulled it from his flesh, the marine never for a moment ceased firing at the attacking planes.

Upon the sinking of his own ship at the beginning of the onslaught, Platoon Sergeant Thomas Hailey of the marines swam to another and assisted in the rescue of his own crew. He then joined a crew manning an anti-aircraft gun and got in some particularly telling shots, even though he had not had previous experience in the use of that particular kind of gun. Later, when he arrived on shore, Sergeant Hailey, clothed only in his underwear and armed only with a rifle, volunteered and went up in an airplane that was leaving on a five-hour search mission!

This was the real spirit of Pearl Harbor.

V

SOME NONCOMBATANTS

Eugene Burns, Associated Press Correspondent, heard the rumbling of guns, but went on with his breakfast until a bomb burst near by.

"Say, something's on!" he said to his wife.

In fifteen minutes they reached town from their Tantalus home. On the way down they had seen the fires at Pearl Harbor. Burns stopped his car on Alakea Street and dashed into the Mutual Telephone building.

"Associated Press, San Francisco! Number's Douglas 6575!"

He picked up more information and details from the telephone girls while he waited for the connection. He wondered whether there would be any answer. If the *Chronicle* had not altered its ways since he left, no reporter would be there at this hour on Sunday.

"Hello!" he yelled, "the Chronicle?" It was. A reporter had come in for his mail. "Swell! Listen, here's a *story!*"

While he was making his dramatic report, a bomb fell on the Schumann Carriage Company a block away, and the explosion was heard over the telephone by the reporter in California.

As he left, the operator said, "I'll bet the mainland papers are going to exaggerate this!"

At Pearl Harbor, M———, a captain's yeoman, and his wife and daughter, were playing with the baby, who was sitting in the middle of the bed. They heard an explosion and decided to pull the bed over by the window, where they could watch the mock raid.

They looked down toward the end of the island. The whole thing seemed on fire. A plane swooped, roaring, over a warship in the harbor. A terrific explosion followed as the plane swooped up again.

"Roberta! run outside and get your brother," Mrs. M——— cried to her daughter.

Roberta ran down the walk to where her little brother and his pal were playing with a small wooden wagon which they had made. As they started back to the house, a plane flew low above them and spattered the sidewalk with machine-gun bullets. The little wagon flew to pieces on the lawn.

M———— went to his post of duty.

A few minutes later a truck swept up to the house.

"Get out of the house! Don't bring anything! Hurry!"

Mrs. M———— and the four children were crowded into the truck of fleeing wives and children. A plane thundered down, strafing. A machine-gun bullet went through the floor of the truck between Mrs. M———— and her eight-year-old boy.

The wild ride ended at a dug-out, where some three hundred persons were collected in safety. From there they could see a dog-fight, probably the one between Rasmussen and the Japanese. Tensely they watched until the Japanese plane fell in flames to the earth. Then the whole crowd cheered.

Cornelia Fort was in the air early that morning. Her pupil, a defense worker, Mr. Suomala, was near the solo stage. They circled John Rodgers airport to make a practise landing. On the down wind leg of their landing, Cornelia noticed a plane coming in from the sea. "An Army bomber," she thought, as she noted its military appearance.

Before her student pilot made the next turn, Cornelia scanned the safety zone they were in to make sure they had the right of way and were clear for the final approach. To her horror, the plane which had but a moment before been far out to sea was now paralyzingly close and headed directly towards them at exactly their same altitude.

Cornelia seized the controls. She jammed the throttle wide open. The plane lurched upward. It barely cleared the wings of the heavy-bellied, oncoming ship. Its roaring motors stunned their ears. For a second it flashed beneath them. The windows of their little training ship rattled violently from the vibration.

"The reckless idiot!" Cornelia exclaimed. She looked down, determined to identify the plane and report the pilot. Instead of the familiar star of the U. S. Army, she saw the fiery circles of the Rising Sun painted clearly on the top of each wing. Incredulously, she looked towards Pearl Harbor. Billowing black oil smoke filled the air. Then she looked at the sky above the harbor, and her spine went rigid. Very high, in perfect formation, a fleet of silver bombers moved soundlessly across the morning sky.* Glistening sticks tumbled out of each bomber

*See Chapter XIV: Historical Notes.

and exploded in the harbor, sending up great fountains of foaming water and debris.

Above the roar of her plane, Cornelia heard the noise of the explosions. "This is it. This is really it!" Cornelia dove the airplane towards the runway. She made a wheel landing not putting the plane's tail down at all as she taxied across to the hangar.

Suddenly the girl pilot felt first fright shake her as gravel spurted in her path and a swift, silent shadow sailed over her.

"Run!" she cried to her student.

As they raced across the field, the student panted plaintively, "When am I going to solo?"

"Not today, Brother!"

At the hangar, despite Cornelia's insistence that she had clearly seen the Rising Sun on the wings of the plane above the field and her assertion that those were Japanese bombs they could hear exploding a quarter of a mile away, no one believed her.

Then, a mechanic from one of the lower hangars came racing up and gasped, "That plane that just flew over here, the son-of-a-bitch shot Bob Tyce!"

The group was stricken with silence. Bob was a flier they had all worked with, eaten with, and flown with every week.

Then Cornelia realized that the bullets aimed at her

—the gravel-spattering bullets—had missed her and killed a friend of hers—the first civilian casualty of the war.

Someone went to help Mrs. Tyce, who had been standing with her husband when he slumped to the concrete ramp. The rest were rooted to the spot, horror-stricken, facing Pearl Harbor. They stared at the fullest wedge of sky they had ever seen. Gun fire shuttled both ways; anti-aircraft bullets streamed upwards and passed torpedoes, bombs, and machine gun fire coming down. Screeching planes catapulted earthward in blinding flames.

As they watched, a Japanese bomber coming in from the sea flew very low, straight towards the hangar where the group stood. They scattered to cover. As they ran, it occurred to several of them that they were possibly the first Americans on American soil to flee from an enemy invader. It left a gritty taste in their mouths.

Johnny Kelly, on duty as life-guard at Barber's Point, looked out over the small bay for fish. A freighter offshore made its slow way along. An airplane flew above it. Suddenly a geyser of water shot up directly behind the ship. A shell landed half a mile from the beach and exploded not far from an early swimmer. Johnny, his friend Erling Hedeman, and four other life-guards talked about calling up head-quarters.

"That kind of war-play is dangerous for swimmers," Johnny said.

The boys climbed up on the water tank the better to see what was going on. Over Pearl Harbor, and out Schofield way, planes were rising like bees from a hive suddenly stirred.

A shell landed on the beach near the water tower, blowing up a *kiawe* tree and leaving a hole about six feet deep. The boys scurried down and collected about ten pounds of souvenir shrapnel. It was so hot they could not hold it.

They cooled the shrapnel and carried it over to Erling's car, watching a formation of planes that appeared. Suddenly one of the planes left the group and dived for them.

"Slick model," Johnny was saying, "look at that N-line engine."

"Hey, look! The Rising Sun!"

When the plane had swooped down so near that they could see the rivets in its side, the Japanese pilot opened fire—pop, pop, pop, pop—all around them. Straight from the propeller the red tracer bullets came for them. Hot lead spattered on the macadam pavement at their feet. One bullet grazed Johnny's head, touching him just lightly enough to leave a pink crease across his brow. The plane swung up and away.

The six boys jumped into the car and started for a safer spot—they thought. Three Japanese planes, attracted to the target, dived for the car. The machine-gun bullets rained upon them. Six husky lads tried to disappear through the floorboard.

Erling raced at sixty in second gear down the highway. He was driving from the floor, and was so crowded he could not shift gears.

Zig-zag they flew down the narrow macadam roadway.

The planes closed in on their tail. Bullets peppered their fenders and the body of the car. They sounded like rocks hitting a zinc washtub.

On the right of the road a clearing appeared, leading to a mango grove. They swerved off the highway and found refuge under the trees.

The car was riddled with holes. The gas tank was punctured, and gas was pouring out. The windshield was shattered.

The boys walked over to the beach, and on the way stopped at the weatherbeaten, two-room shack of Nick the Hawaiian. His feet propped up on the wall of his porch, Nick was reading an old detective magazine. Without taking his feet down, he said,

"Hey, whassamatta? I live on dis beach forty-fi' year I never hear so much noise. No can read anymo'. I think bimeby I move from here!"

In the midst of the attack, R. H. Lodge, plantation overseer, was standing under a gnarled monkeypod tree on Waipio peninsula, just opposite Ford Island. One of the ships, with a direct hit, brought down a Japanese plane. It landed with a shattering crash by the water's edge, but, amazingly, did not burst into flames.

Lodge dashed over to it. There on the ground lay the Japanese pilot—scalped. The oversear looked up, and there a few feet above his head, on a bough of a huge *kiawe* tree was a complete scalp of bristly black hair. In his swift, uncontrolled descent, the Japanese had crashed through the tree and a broken branch had peeled off the top of his head as neatly as if an Indian had done the job with a hunter's knife.

For a moment, Lodge looked with a collector's eye on the scalp, but this was one trophy he hadn't the stomach to take. He turned away and picked up the pilot's machine gun belt instead.

James Duncan is an amateur flyer, and belongs to the flying club, *Hui Lele*. There are twenty members who take time about with a plane. He had signed up for it on Sunday in order to get some instruction from Tommy Tomerlin, who gives lessons to the *Hui Lele* members when he can find time from his duties as co-pilot for Inter-Island Airways.

In compliance with club rules, the two men wrote down the time they left the airport: 7:55. Taking their time, they flew past Pearl Harbor, over the orderly flying fields of Hickam and Wheeler, and landed at Haleiwa, making a few practice landings there. They flew on to Kahuku and made some more landings on the emergency field there. Continuing on their way around the island, they passed over the Mormon Temple, famous show place and admired it from the air. They had just flown over it when hell broke loose. Streams of red lead suddenly came cutting across them from two directions.

Two planes were attacking them, one from above in front, one from above at the side. The one from the front was diving on them. Red tracer bullets were shooting at them, some hitting the cockpit and cutting through the fuselage. The first attacking plane swept past the tail of their plane. It was followed immediately by the second attacker, which passed just over them. Their little "cub" plane trembled and shook in the wake of the swift, heavy bombers.

In the excitement, neither Duncan nor Tomerlin had identified the planes. The only explanation for the attack that they could think of was that they might have flown too near a military reservation, and were getting a warning. It seemed a bit severe, especially when they saw that the first plane had made a chandelle and was heading for them again, tracer bullets flashing in a line from the attacking plane toward theirs.

In the next five minutes they were attacked three times, by both planes. When they finally did see the Rising Sun on the wings and tails of the planes, Tomerlin headed as fast as he could go for the steep mountain cliffs that follow the sea a part of the way on this side of the island. Flying very low above the water, only about fifty feet, and very close in to the jagged edge of the mountainside, they found cover.

The Japanese bombers were so heavy and fast that they did not have sufficient distance in which to attack and still come out of their dives.

Tomerlin approached the Kaneoche air base, flying out to sea in accordance with military regulations as they passed it. Clouds of black smoke hung in the air above the base. Geysers of water were leaping into the air from fifty to a hundred feet, thrown up by bombs aimed at planes anchored on the water.

The two men wanted to head straight across the mountain range for home, but it was not a clear day, and clouds were hanging low, in some places halfway down the mountainside. Then they saw a triangle of light shining through a gap. They gained altitude and headed for the triangle. They forgot all warnings and flew close to the ragged edges of the cliffs. On any other day they would have considered that hitting the triangle was a delicate flying problem. Now they entered it bodily, skimming along only eight or ten feet above the tops of the guava bushes in order to avoid going into the cloud above. The violent air currents of the *pali* gave them a fillip and sent them on their way.

Once through, they came upon the whole panorama of the Japanese attack. Airplanes in formations of fourteen or fifteen winged their even flight over Pearl Harbor. Bombs like glittering schools of silver fish came raining down. They fell swiftly, steadily. A great rumbling shook the earth, and tremendous clouds of black oil smoke shot upward.

Stray planes were having it out in dog-fights over the sea. Other strays were circling and strafing the airports. Hickam and Wheeler showed the effects of the raid. Chaos had taken the place of the order which Duncan had admired on the way out an hour before.

As they approached their home field, the John Rodgers Airport, they saw that it was being strafed by enemy planes. The landing ground was cleared. All the planes were spread out to the four edges of the airport, spread wide apart. They were loath to land, but they wanted no more attacks from the air, so down they went.

As they circled to land, a car rushed out of the hangar where they kept their plane. It reached them just as their wheels touched the ground, and, racing alongside their plane, the driver of the car screamed, "Park that thing in the weeds and run for your life! The Japs are attacking us!"

Tomerlin ran the plane to the outer edge of the field and stopped. The two leaped out and started running for the hangar, directly across the open space. Duncan suddenly stopped, turned, and ran back to the plane for his hat.

Inside the hangar they were nervous, and decided it would be safer to get off the airfield entirely. They ran for their car and set out in it down the road leading to the main highway. But the Japanese were strafing roads leading to the port; so they abandoned the car. They dove under a house just as a Japanese strafing plane shot across the sky above them. Shingles flew from the roof, popped off by the machine-gun bullets.

Duncan and Tomerlin crawled out and started home on foot. Down the highway they were picked up by a truck and taken in to town.

On Monday Duncan's telephone rang. It was the secretary of *Hui Lele*.

"Say, Duncan, you're being fined, you know."

"No. Why?"

"You didn't check in your time when you and Tomerlin got back to the airport yesterday."

There were at least three Hawaiians whom the Japanese literally did not disturb in the least.

The wife of a Navy officer at Ford Island is a very talented painter. Her husband was away on duty. She had a picture to finish, and she was working on it so intently on Sunday morning that she did not notice that the "practice" bombing was being done by our neighbors from Tokyo. All through the raid she painted. If the truck driver whose duty it was to evacuate wives and children from her block stuck his head in at the door and yelled at her, she did not hear him.

The next afternoon she went out for a walk. A patrol guard stopped her.

"What are you doing here?"

"I'm taking a walk."

"You know we can't permit anyone to be here!"

"Why not?"

So it went until she discovered that she had painted through the most terrible catastrophe suffered in the Hawaiian Islands in over a hundred years—without knowing it.

The biggest news story of the year was on the wires. Harlan Reynolds heard it in New York over the radio. He picked up the telephone and dictated a cable to his maiden aunts at Waikiki.

At eleven-thirty the same morning it was delivered to them.

DEEPEST SYMPATHY DEAR AUNTS PLEASE COME HOME IMMEDIATELY.

"What in the world is the matter with Harlan?" they asked each other in bewilderment.

The news had made headlines in the New York papers, but it had not reached the ladies at their knitting in Waikiki.

VI

THE WOUNDED

The Navy

THE FIRST CASUALTIES TO COME IN WERE THOSE WHO were able to bring themselves. Men covered with oil and burns struggled ashore. A captain was with them, oil-covered, most of his clothing torn off. His admiral and superior officer had been killed. Just before the wounded stragglers reached the Naval Hospital, a Japanese bomber with three men in it fell from the sky, bounced off the concrete hospital building, cut a palm tree in two, and crashed in flames on the asphalt tennis court.

Hospital staff men at first were not disturbed by the noise of the enemy planes streaking across the sky. The Naval Hospital is directly opposite the Ford

Island Air Station, from which planes were taking off all the time and dynamite had been used for several days for blasting near the hospital. But within five minutes of the time that twenty Japanese planes screeched over the hospital buildings, the stations for air attack were manned in the operating suite and in the ward dressing rooms.

As the Japanese swept in from the sea, flying no more than fifty feet off the ground, skirting the hospital, the convalescent patients were hastily evacuated to temporary quarters outside to make room for the injured men who began coming in on stretchers. One young seaman had been hit on the side of the head above his ear by a piece of flying shrapnel. It drove into his skull behind his right ear and came out above his eye—out of his skull, but not his head. Lodged beneath the unbroken skin of his forehead, it bulged like a great knot. A machine gun had sprayed his stomach with lead. "We'll do what we can," the doctor said. The young seaman is alive to tell the tale.

Another youthful sailor came walking in with his whole lower face shot away—no upper lip or chin. He wanted to shake hands with everyone. He tried to talk, but his tongue only made noises against the roof of his mouth. "We were there together, fellows," is what he wanted to say. They buried him two days later.

Medical Officer Captain Reynolds Hayden looked up from a wounded man and saw a Japanese plane ablaze fly directly toward the front of the main hospital building. It swerved to the left, struck the corner of the laboratory building and crashed in flames on the chief petty officers' quarters. Hospital fire fighters rushed to extinguish the fire, but the quarters, a small frame building, were practically destroyed. Two Japanese aviators in the plane were killed instantly.

Now the ambulances arrived. In they came, bringing the crippled, the burned. Swiftly, carefully, the litter bearers and the ambulance teams worked. They saved the lives of countless wounded by bringing them in during the "golden hours" before infection set in.

Numbers of young seamen had lost arms or legs, but hundreds were burned—burned from the sheets of flaming oil which had enveloped them on the battleships, and burned again from the lake of fire into which they had dived.

Each wounded man was immediately given morphine to relieve his suffering the moment one of the medical officers or hospital corpsmen reached him. All the attendants were armed with previously prepared units of the pain-relieving medicine in the form of morphine "syrettes"—small plastic flasks equipped with hypodermic needles, containing a single dose of the morphine solution. The syrettes saved precious minutes; there was no time for the preparation of hypodermic needles or solutions. Medical attendants plunged swift hands into their "battle bags" for the syrettes, quickly removed the protecting tube from the needle, and injected the wounded with one-half grain of morphine. "A few minutes, and agony would fade from their faces," Captain W. A. Michael said.

Many of the "flash burns" followed the outline of the sailors' clothing. The faces, arms, and legs of those men wearing only undershirts and shorts were severely burned. Those not wearing undershirts suffered in addition agonizing burns on their chests and backs. Men fully clothed received only face and hand burns from the explosive blasts. When the call to General Quarters had sounded, many men rushed out to their battle stations without waiting to dress. Some who died in the hospital from extensive body burns probably would have lived had they been wearing more clothes at the time they were injured.

The burned came in such numbers—sixty per cent of all wounds were burns—that doctors had to utilize any atomizer that was available to spray soothing solutions on the burned men's bodies. Ordinary Flit

guns were emptied, immediately refilled with medicated liquid, and used to spray the wounds of the
injured.

Some of the men suffered burns and blisters which
covered as much as half of the total surface of their
bodies. They needed blood plasma and plenty of it.
Their own plasma—the watery portion of their blood
—was rushing to the blistered areas of their bodies
to protect the tender flesh under the skin. It was drain-
ing, by the quart, out of the piteously burned men.
Tireless Navy doctors literally pumped gallons of new
plasma into the men's veins to replace what they
had lost.

While doctors worked they watched carefully
to guard against the dreaded signs of traumatic shock.
They had learned from bitter World War I experience
how even superficial burns and wounds can cause
fatal reactions. With them, preventing shock took
precedence over all other treatments except the control of hemorrhage. As the seamen lost plasma, less
of their blood could circulate. The doctors knew that
the red blood cells would remain in the men's blood
until the last stage of shock, when the inner linings
of their smallest blood vessels would be severely
damaged by the prolonged absence of oxygen. And
the doctors also knew that when that happened death

would come to these seamen—unless they received the precious plasma which would provide a vehicle for the circulation of the red blood cells which was so necessary to overcome the oxygen deficiency in the tissues.

The new sulfa drugs united with the plasma to provide one of medicine's most effective weapons against the casualties of war. Generous doses of sulfathiazole were given by mouth to stop invading germs before they could do further damage. Injured men were grateful for large, cool dressings which were dipped into a mixture of mineral oil and sulfanilamide or sulfathiazole and applied directly to their burned bodies. The smooth oil soothed the throbbing flesh; the sulfa drugs prevented infection.

Only the most seriously wounded—those demanding immediate surgical attention—could be sent directly to the operating amphitheatre at the Naval Hospital where surgical teams worked in ceaseless relays. The other wounded had to wait—and, in their cases the miracle drug, sulfanilamide, dusted into severe abdominal or intestinal wounds, prevented fatal infection from setting in.

The spirit of the boys was unbelievable. The most impressive fact about the hospital, filled with wounded, many suffering unto death, was the silen.

of the place. No confusion—no unnecessary clamor —no crying out. You never heard "Oh, that *hurts!*" Instead, they said, "Watch that leg, please, ma'am. It's broken in two places." Neither nurses, chaplains, nor doctors heard a murmur of complaint.

In an hour boys had become men, and men heroes. The medical officer walked down a row of wounded to select the one to receive immediate treatment. His trained eye at once saw the most serious case. He went directly to a young boy. Burned skin was dripping off the youth's entire upper body.

"Take care of my buddy, here, Doc," the boy said. "He's hurt lots worse than I am."

That sentence was spoken more often than any other throughout the day—"Take care of my buddy." Boys who were much worse off than their neighbors asked nurses for water for their buddies, and said to the chaplains, "Padre, see if you can't find a doctor right away. My buddy's in terrible shape. He's been lying here ten minutes now."

Mrs. Ernest Dunlap heard that her husband, a Navy lieutenant, was wounded. She went to the hospital and a nurse led her through a silent ward. At the end of a row of cots they stopped. Before them lay a man with his face charred black and deeply gashed. His cheek bone was fractured and his jaw was broken in several places. Mrs. Dunlap did not recognize her own husband. Then he tried to smile. The first words she heard him say were, "I can see and hear. And I'll be in there again before long."

At the rate of a man a minute for sixteen hours the terribly burned and wounded men were cared for. Every available cot, nurse, and doctor was busy. One Navy doctor, who was a convalescent patient following a major operation undergone long before December 7th, gave up his cot and worked, helping to care for the wounded steadily until he became exhausted. Other convalescent patients joined the teams of hospital corpsmen and helped to dress wounds, prepare soothing solutions, and administer intravenous medication. A group of patients, too weak to move about, equipped flashlights with blue paper and blue glass to be used in the coming night, when the only light in the blacked-out wards would be a faint glow, lest a gleam guide the Japanese to another attack.

The Naval Hospital was filled in a hurry, overflowing to the outdoors, to the plantation hospitals, and to emergency stations. Two hundred cots were set up in the uncompleted buildings of Mobile Base Hospital Number 2 on the hill behind Pearl Harbor, and other hundreds at the well-equipped Submarine

Base dispensary and the Naval Air Station sick bay, even though it had been bombed.

A hundred cots were set up in the yard of the Officer's Club, where the medical personnel of the sunken minelayer *Oglala* set up operating facilities, assisted by doctors and trained hospital corpsmen of gutted ships. The medical officer of the doomed *Argonne* directed the operating crews and supervised the dressing station on the porch, where minor injuries were treated.

There, lesser burns were relieved by the application of the old stand-by, tannic acid. In some cases dressings were dipped in gun tubs filled with tannic acid solution and then placed gently on the wounds.

While the strafing continued, Chaplain Strauss set up a seventy-five-bed emergency hospital in an unfinished barracks near the harbor. As each wave of planes came over, the attendants dropped to the floor. Tensely the men and women worked. Another wave came, and all went down, Chaplain Strauss with them. In the silence they heard the sound of a terrific rip. The chaplain's trouser-knee had split. When there was a lull, he rang up the Supply Department and asked them to leave a needle and some thread the next time someone came by. Soon a special worker came whipping in with five hundred spools of thread and a hundred needles.

"Hey," one of the wounded men said, "whaddye think the Padre wears—a tent?"

THE ARMY

Meanwhile, medical miracles were being performed at Tripler General Hospital, where the Army's wounded were taken. Again, the spirit of these American boys was thrilling to see. Their wounds were even worse than those of the burned. Some of them were too terrible to describe. They were mortal wounds by the side of which the loss of an arm or leg was minor. Dr. King put in an emergency call to the doctors of Honolulu for surgical teams. By a rare coincidence, at the very moment of his appeal virtually every surgeon in Honolulu was present at the Mabel Smythe auditorium, listening to an address being delivered by Dr. John J. Moorhead, world-famous specialist in traumatic surgery. His lecture was suddenly interrupted when the door to the auditorium flew open.

"Ten surgeons are wanted at once at Tripler General Hospital!" shouted Dr. Phillips.

Fifty physicians rushed for the door, Dr. Moorhead among them, but not before he had carefully picked up a small radio-like instrument which was on the lecture table waiting to serve as Exhibit A in the day's address on "War Wounds." He and Dr. Strode leaped into an automobile and wove through Honolulu's narrow streets, crowded with station wagons, trucks, and autos. They dashed between taxis by the hundred which were rushing officers, soldiers, and sailors to their battle stations at Pearl Harbor.

On the steps of the Army hospital they were met by the Commanding Officer Miller.

"The operating room is upstairs. Please hurry."

Soon twelve surgical teams were working as fast as the wounded could be brought into the four emergency hospital rooms. And in they came—a hundred, two hundred, three hundred, and more—before it was over. It was a sight the like of which none of the surgeons had ever seen before.

A Japanese bomb had made a direct hit on the new mess hall at Hickam Field while hundreds of young aviators were seated there at breakfast. Now, maimed and bleeding, they were brought, tight-lipped, uncomplaining, to the doctors.

The stretcher-bearers laid before the surgeons men with arms and legs shot off, men with shell fragments penetrating their abdomens and even their spinal columns and heads. Some had stomachs and chests blown away, and one flight lieutenant who had been sprayed by a Japanese machine gunner had twenty-three holes in his intestines. Men that day endured fractures so severe and wounds so ragged that none of their surgeons had ever seen their equal except in the dissecting room. Dr. Moorhead had been in charge of evacuation hospitals for the wounded at Chateau Thierry and the Argonne, but he said, "I had never before seen so many cases of such gravity come into any hospital in such a short period of time."

But all the time the ambulance teams and litter bearers were bringing in the wounded and while they waited together for treatment, not one moan or whimper escaped them.

The doctors were amazed and inspired by the sight. In cases of this sort, they are accustomed to hear the most agonized shrieks and groans. They expected a madhouse. They found boys living up to the code of professional soldiers—to lie still and cause no more disturbance than necessary. They were not unconscious. They were alert, calmly waiting, and fully conscious of what they had gone through. There was not even any profanity. Nurses and chaplains moved among them, comforting the wounded and attending the dying.

A nurse put her hand behind the head of a blond boy of twenty, who had a serious chest wound, touched his lips with a glass of water. He took a swallow, smiled into her eyes, and said, "Thank you." They were his last words.

If spirit was high in the waiting line, in the surgical wards it was heroic. The whole experience of the morning seemed to act as a powerful anesthetic. The men did not seem to know that their bodies were in agony, undergoing such pain as often kills people from its shock alone. They were just out of action.

On young Lieutenant Miller, there was no time to make a finished amputation, carefully moving the skin back above the line of amputation and then folding it over the stump when the operation was completed. His leg had to have attention, quick. Dr. Halford made a straight guillotine amputation—the kind that leaves a big stump and painful nerves exposed. When the stout lieutenant came back to have the wound dressed, a most excruciating operation, he tightened his lips, held on to the table, and stood the pain without a murmur. His example was repeated many times.

"Are you afraid?" the surgeon often asked.

"Not at all. Go ahead!" was always the reply.

One man said, "Just hurry up. I want to get back to my battle station!"

In the operating rooms every table was kept busy. The medical officer moved swiftly among the wounded, designating the order in which the cases should be treated. Hospital corpsmen and nurses were constantly on the lookout for means of accelerating the movement of patients into and out of the operating room. All was quiet and non-theatrical. It was the silence of courage.

Only once was there any faltering. As a young nurse was about to administer an anesthetic to a wounded soldier, a burst of anti-aircraft flak fell with a crash on the roof above the operating room. The nurse started to faint, and fell against Dr. Moorhead's arm. As the doctor braced her, he said, "Steady. The English can take it. The Chinese can take it. And so can we!" Immediately, the nurse pulled herself together, and resolutely resumed the administration of the anesthetic.

After the wounded had been given morphine to check their pain and sulfa drugs to prevent infection, then came debridement. Every bit of dead and dying flesh that could give food for germs was cut away and ounces of priceless sulfanilimide powder were sifted into the wound.

The surgeons were grateful for the identification tags around each boy's neck, showing, among other things, his blood type. Precious time was lost whenever a patient had to wait to have his blood typed so that transfusion could be made. These boys *needed* blood. They were so seriously wounded that they were as likely to die from the shock as from the wounds themselves. In such cases, a patient will be talking, and suddenly die. At Tripler, the surgeons pumped quarts and gallons of rich, life-sustaining blood and plasma into the veins of the soldiers, relieving them from the shock of their wounds and preparing them for the coming ordeal of surgery.

The surgeons were also deeply grateful that an invaluable surgical instrument—the Berman Foreign-Body Locator—had been brought to Honolulu by Dr. Moorhead *just four days before the attack*. On December 7th it was the only instrument of its kind in the world and in all the world there was one spot where it was most desperately needed. This tiny spot was here, far off in the middle of the Pacific ocean, but providentially the Locator was in Hawaii to do its time-saving, pain-saving, and life-saving work.

The almost magical electro-magnetic power box looks like a small table radio. In it is mounted a radio frequency circuit from which extends a movable coil which ends in a steel pointer about half an inch in diameter and twelve inches long. As the probe in the surgeon's hand approaches a piece of metal, the presence of the foreign substance is registered on the "radio." One highly sensitive dial tunes in on iron fragments, and another on steel and all other metals.

The flexible pointer of the Locator can be passed above or around the wound in two planes at right angles to each other. At the two points of greatest deflection the surgeon makes pencil marks on the flesh. Where the projection of these two points meet, he will find the metal. If he makes an incision and misses the fragment, he can introduce the sterilized steel probe directly into the wound, even if it is in the lung, abdomen, or brain. A small extension of the incision brings him to the metal. Bullets, shrapnel, steel splinters, and bomb fragments were located at once at Tripler, using the Locator, minimizing the shock and agony which have long been the horror of surgical probing.

A bomb fragment had pierced a young soldier's thigh. Dr. Moorhead bent over the wounded man on the white operating table and passed the slender, shining pointer of the Locator over the gaping flesh wound. As the pointer approached the torn flesh, the needle on the dial trembled and began to register —1—2—3—getting warm—4—5—6—no mistake— 7—here it is! Deftly the surgeon marked the spot indicated by the dial. Unerringly guesswork eliminated, he made a swift incision and immediately lifted out a jagged piece of shrapnel. No probing, no painful searching, no delay. Time and again, loss of valuable time was avoided by the use of this new "magic wand" of surgery.

The Japanese sprayed plenty of machine gun lead into the bodies of fighting men that day, and in several instances the Locator was the only means of finding those bullets. In one case, surgeons near Dr. Moorhead depended upon the usual means of locating a bullet lodged behind a young lieutenant's collar bone. X-ray pictures were made, but when the surgeons plotted their incisions according to the revelations of the films, they found that the bullet had moved away from its original position. They resorted to driving a "landmark" needle down towards the spot where they thought the bullet rested, and new X-ray pictures were taken. These showed the bullet's position in relation to the needle, but when the doctors made another incision, they discovered that during the time the X-ray pictures were being developed, the bullet had moved again. The offending metal was finally found after a long period of time. In a similar case, by using the Locator, the surgeons removed a bullet in less than ten minutes.

Late in the morning a young man was brought in. Pinned to his chest was a red card marked "Urgent." His right leg was paralyzed by a bullet which had lodged in his spinal column.

"It won't do you any good to operate, Doc," the young fighter said. "You can't find the bullet 'way back there."

"Do you want to bet?" Dr. Moorhead asked.

"Okay—a quarter."

Some time later, Dr. Moorhead placed the bullet in his young patient's hand. The next day, in the ward, the soldier stopped him, reached under his pillow and held out a twenty-five cent piece. "I'll be back on duty soon," he said with a smile, "and here's your quarter, because a soldier always pays his debts!"

An Army doctor, a New Yorker, watched Dr. Moorhead remove a piece of shrapnel from a soldier's leg. "Well," he said, as the surgeon handed him the retrieved metal, "for all we know, that may be a piece of our Sixth Avenue El!"

As each boy—most of them were twenty-one— came out of the anesthetic, one of the first things he said was, "Let me see what hit me."

Dr. Moorhead gave a small metallic fragment to one young man just awakening and said to him, "Made in Japan." The boy turned it over in his hand

and looked at it for a minute. "Don't worry," he said. "They'll get it back."

The combination of brave, patient wounded, excellent nurses, and outstanding surgeons administering the most modern treatment for war wounds made Pearl Harbor a sweeping medical victory. Infection, which in World War I killed eighty per cent of the men suffering abdominal wounds alone, hardly occurred in Hawaii. Not a single loss of arm or leg was necessary because of post-surgical infection. Even among men whose wounds had been contaminated by the fertilizer-dirty soil of Hickam and Wheeler Fields, and who had their wounds merely coated with sulfanilimide and left undebrided for the first twenty-four hours, not a single serious infection set in. In the struggle against what Dr. Moorhead, one of the heroes of the day, has called "the Four Horsemen of Trauma—Death, Disability, Deformity, and Despair" —the action at Pearl Harbor was one of the world's greatest medical and surgical victories in any war! *

*See Chapter XIV: Historical Notes.

VII

BLOOD BANK

WE LEARNED IN HONOLULU THAT SUNDAY HOW narrow the dividing line is between soldier and civilian in war time. We were inspired by the example of America's courageous soldiers and sailors, and fighting mad at the Japanese invaders for their cowardly attack. We wanted to do something. There was vitally important work to do, and civilians leaped to it.

Soon after the bombing started, a call came into the headquarters of the Hawaii Medical Association. It just said, "Pearl Harbor! Ambulance! For God's sake, hurry!"

This was the challenge that the Medical Corps had been waiting for from the day, months ago, when they first organized. And did they pick it up! Within only twenty minutes from the time the call came, the doctors and volunteer workers of the medical units had stripped the interiors of over one hundred laundry trucks, lumber trucks, and delivery trucks of every description, equipped them neatly with previously prepared frames containing room for four litters each, and were speeding to the scene of action. One unit arrived early enough to receive a souvenir piece of shrapnel, flung at them by a Japanese bomb.

When the shooting started, Mrs. William Moir, chairman of the American Red Cross Motor Corps, was in the midst of it. She was swimming at Punaluu on the other side of the island when machine-gun bullets splashed the water around her. She looked up and saw a dog-fight going on in deadly earnest directly above her. She ran ashore. As she slammed her house door behind her, a plane with the Rising Sun on its wing-tips fell into the deep water off-shore.

When Mrs. Moir reached town, her motor corps was hitting on all eight. Nearly one hundred women were out on the road. Every available sedan, roadster, and banana-wagon was carrying men to Pearl Harbor. Driving on this three-lane highway was no job for a weakling. It has been a bottleneck of traffic ever since travel to and from the defense areas has put such heavy demands upon it. On that memorable Sunday it was an inferno. Army trucks, official and unofficial emergency wagons, ambulances, Red Cross and Motor Corps cars, and hundreds of taxis, rushing officers and men to their battle stations literally screamed up and down the six-mile road.

The Motor Corps women were equal to the task.

Dr. Pinkerton, making his rounds at Queen's Hospital, heard a commotion below in Emergency. He stepped to the balcony and looked down. Dozens of cases were coming in all at once—mutilations and burns. As the Doctor rushed back into the hospital to give instructions, an emergency call came from Tripler Hospital.

"Blood plasma, quick!"

In five minutes Dr. Pinkerton was at the refrigeration plant of the Hawaiian Electric Company where the local blood bank was stored. There were 210 flasks of 250 cc.—half pint. He rushed sixty of these to Queen's Emergency for the civilian cases coming in and sped on to Tripler with the rest.

The call came from Pearl Harbor: "Plasma!"

The precious fluid was divided and part was hurried to the surgeons at the Harbor. It was going fast.

At eleven o'clock that morning Dr. Pinkerton made a short appeal over the raido. He did not say how badly plasma was needed. He did not explain what it is, or tell how a young lieutenant's life had

just been saved by its use. Getting his breath back
after running up three long flights of stairs at KGU,
all he said was, "A call for Volunteer blood donors!
Report immediately to Queen's Hospital!"

In half an hour, five hundred people were waiting
at the doors of the hospital. The staff of doctors and
trained technicians, some fifteen in all, were at work
at twelve tables, but they could not take the blood
as fast as it was offered. Some persons stood in line for
seven hours to give their blood. Most of them did not
know what blood plasma is, but they knew they were
helping.

The crowd of blood donors was a thrilling mass
response to the dastardly Japanese attack. This waiting line was an amazing thing. Here were Honolulu's
masses, a unique amalgam in the history of the world
—a people who do not communicate with each other
except on the level of pidgin English, but a people
emotionally united. Honolulu society women stood
in line or sat on benches by the wall beside the city's
great good-humored lower classes. A well-known
woman painter, a wife of a corporation president, and
a water-front washwoman waited together and indig-
nantly agreed on "what a treacherous thing it was."
Japanese by the hundreds were there, many of them
members of the Oahu Citizens for Home Defense

Committee. Some older, alien Japanese were there too, dressed in black, which they traditionally wear on occasions where respect is due. They stood in attitudes of infinite patience, waiting to register a silent protest with their blood. A Portuguese blind boy of nineteen and his blind sister three years younger were there, brought in by their mother. They had heard the call over the radio and insisted that she bring them down.

Defense workers came in their dirty work clothes, got preference in the line, gave their blood, and went back to work. Welders came with eyes red and burning. They gave their blood, and back they went to the job. Large groups of employees came straight from work in buses provided by the companies. The beds had to be protected with newspapers to save the sheets from oil, canefield dirt, and the red soil of the pineapple fields with which the workers were covered.

A bunch of huge Hawaiians came lumbering in from the Honolulu Iron Works. Dirty and oily, when they leaned against the wall, they left big smudges. They were all taken into the same room for their lettings. They laughed and joked, teasing a Puerto Rican among them who was scared. "Wait till you get that shot of brandy at the end of the line, boy. You feel numba one swell!" they told him. The average extraction was about 400 cc., or something less than a pint. Several of these Hawaiians gave 750 cc. and went back to their job at the Iron Works.

A Dutch ship was in port for only a few hours. The entire crew came up to give their blood.*Numbers of passengers came, too. Six big husky Dutch women came in a group. They were very welcome, for one of the things the doctors discovered was that a pint of woman's blood gives more plasma than a pint of man's. The Dutch sextet yielded generous quantities of plasma-rich blood.

Whole families came at once. The preferable age limits were from eighteen to fifty, but young boys lied and old men asserted their rights in order to be included in the line. The Hon. Walter F. Frear, former Governor of the Territory, and Mrs. Frear went down. He is seventy-eight and she is seventy-two. When it was suggested that they might be too old, Mrs. Frear said, "It ought to be very good blood. It has lasted us a long time!" "I should say so," said Mrs. Sarah Wilder, grandmother of grown men. "My blood is better than that of half of these young whippersnappers!"

To the hospital came a letter by special messenger from a long-time resident. It said in effect: "I realize that I am eighty-one, and that the request was for

*See Chapter XIV: Historical Notes.

younger people. I am strong and healthy. However, I am very heavy and cannot stand long at a time without great fatigue. It will save me two trips to the hospital if you will permit me to make an appointment. My daughter will bring me down." And she added, "I may say that from what I have seen of this war so far, it is nothing like as bad as Custer's was in '76."

There was one Hawaiian woman who was so big that the doctors had to give up. In the depths of fat they could not find her vein. One seaman's wife had veins too small, and was rejected. Corps of Honolulu police and firemen made up for these, swelling the bank with averages well over 600 cc. each.

At the end of the line, each donor who wanted it was given a generous shot of good brandy. The policemen accused each other of coming in because of the finishing draught. The beach-boys pretended to be quite faint and were given long pulls on the bottle to revive them.

A surprising number of girls who are following Sadie Thompson's footsteps in the South Seas showed up in the line. And four of them, after donating their blood, asked to help further. They got a job washing tubing, the dirtiest, smelliest, meanest of all laboratory jobs. They worked hard and stayed at it as long as anyone.

Many donors came back. One second-class seaman was recognized by a nurse.

"You shouldn't come back so soon," she warned him.

"My brother was killed," he said. "I want to do something."

That's what everyone in Hawaii was saying—"I want to do something."

VIII

THE RESCUE

OUT IN PEARL HARBOR, SOON AFTER THE SECOND attack, the *Oklahoma* had settled on its side, lying like a great whale, almost totally submerged. Some members of a rescue party in a motor launch passing near the great hulk happened to hear the faint sound of tapping coming from somewhere in the bowels of the capsized ship. There were men, alive, trapped in the battleship! This was reported to yard officers at eleven o'clock in the morning and immediately a crew of workers with acetylene cutters was dispatched.

They opened holes in the outer shell astern and midship, trying to get through. Amidships they cut through the hull into a fire room where they had heard voices and knew the imprisoned men were still alive. After several hours of gruelling work it was found that the danger from fire and excessive smoke was so great that the acetylene cutting method had to be abandoned.

Julio DeCastro, Hawaiian-born, a master "leading-man," caulker, and chipper, took out with a crew of experts with pneumatic cutting equipment—a slower but safer method. They, twenty-one in all, went aft and drilled a small test hole. Fresh water under high pressure spurted out, drenching the workmen. They had luckily drilled into a fresh water tank, a good place from which to launch the drilling through to the men inside.

They began with renewed energy to cut out a hole large enough to admit them to the tank. It was dark by now. The *Arizona*, still burning, illuminated the entire Harbor silhouetting the crew on the hull of the ship and lighting up their work for them. About nine o'clock anti-aircraft guns from all over the harbor opened up on a lone Japanese plane which had apparently missed its carrier and been left behind. For an hour the flak from the anti-aircraft guns filled the sky.* It shot all around DeCastro and the crew at work, but they disregarded their own danger. They only hoped that the men caught inside were not suffocating, but they knew that water was prob-

*See Chapter XIV: Historical Notes.

ably rising in the compartments. When the anti-air-craft fire got too hot around the workmen's heads, they flattened out against the exposed hull for a minute, with nothing but their prayers to protect them.

The drilling of the hole finished, more precious time was used in pumping the water out of the storage tank. When most of it had been pumped out, De-Castro and two others dropped down into it. There they had a second stroke of luck. Right below them was a manhole. That meant they could use that opening and not be forced to spend valuable time in drilling another man-sized hole.

The manhole lid could not be raised from their side, but by drilling a small hole in just the right place, DeCastro was able to put his arm through, undo the hatch from the under side, and lay it open. He flashed a light through the aperture into the next compartment. It was dry and painted white. This was a void, and he knew that on the other side of it they would find the men who had been signaling.

They dropped down into the chasm and found themselves standing on a deck. They searched until they found another hatch, knelt down close to it, and shouted. Someone on the other side shouted back—shouted with a joy that was good to hear.

"Are you all right?" DeCastro cried.

"Yeah, so far, but the water is coming up faster now! It's up to our waists already!" one man cried back.

Other men shouted, "For God's sake hurry up!" "Cut us out!" "Burn through this hatch!"

DeCastro calmed them. "Keep steady, boys, and listen to what I am going to tell you: Now, just one of you, one who's strong and well—you do all the talking. The rest of you keep quiet and don't lose your heads!"

The spirit of the men was inspiring. It was early Monday morning. For twenty-four hours they had been in that black horror without light, food, sleep, or any assurance that help was coming. Yet after the first excited outburst they quieted down and followed directions.

Instructions had to be obeyed to the split second. As DeCastro and his men opened the hull, pressures inside were constantly changing. The air pressure had kept the water down and prevented the boys inside from drowning, but now that the rescue crew was letting in air which released the pressure, the water inside the hull would rise fast.

Finally the last dogs were off and the last hatch thrown open. Six strapping seamen came rushing out of their prison, naked as the day they were born. In their frantic scramble they knocked DeCastro down. He floundered in the water, but it was a pleasure for him. He thoroughly enjoyed seeing those young men rush out of their black hell hole.

It was six o'clock Monday morning. The rescuers heard more tapping. It came from behind the far bulkhead of the compartment they had just opened. DeCastro, followed by two helpers, climbed into the compartment from which they had just freed the six sailors, waded to the bulkhead opposite, and shouted. An answering sailor yelled back, "Hurry up, can't you? The water's coming up fast. Some of the short guys have to hang onto the overhead in here!"

DeCastro said he never knew how slow chipping a hole could be. The water steadily rose in his compartment. He knew it was rising on the sailors on the other side, although they never complained. When the hole was cut through, and light again shone in the pitch blackness of the prison, the water swirled around the men's armpits. Eleven men streaked out of the hole like bolts of lightning.

By this time DeCastro had had enough—the water was pouring in on them.

"Let's get out, fast!" he shouted to his men.

"I can't find my chipper," one objected.

"To hell with that chipper and everything else! Let's get out of here!" DeCastro yelled.

As the last workman crawled through the hatch to safety, the compartment was completely filled with tons of heavy seawater. It rose all the way to the ceiling.

The *Oklahoma* is a big ship, and men were caught in more than one section of it. The wary rescuers reached eight more sailors after boring through an oil tank. DeCastro and two others dropped down onto the floor of the fume-permeated tank. As they crossed the slippery floor, one of the men heard knocking under his feet. DeCastro yelled through a covered manhole, "Take patience, now. We'll get you all out. There's a lot of pressure in there, so watch your ears. I'm going to release the pressure before I open this manhole!"

"Okay, okay," answered the sailors.

"Now listen. When I get this hatch open, the weakest and the injured should come out first. The strongest should come out last."

"Okay, okay."

There was a testing hole in the manhole cover and DeCastro opened it, covering it tightly with his hands to ease the pressure off slowly. When the pressure

was off he shouted to the trapped men telling them
to undo the manhole cover.

And did they go to work on it!

They leaped out in a hurry, also unencumbered
with clothes after thirty-six hours in their dungeon.
One had a broken finger, another a broken arm.

"What time is it?" one asked.

"Monday."

"Hell, I lost a day," he answered. "I thought it
was still Sunday!"

In all, thirty-two men were saved from the rising
water in the capsized *Oklahoma*, one rescue crew
penetrating one hundred and fifty feet into the hull to
free the trapped sailors. Two, the last to be liberated,
were released from the forward section of the hull
about one o'clock Tuesday.

It was seven o'clock Monday night when De-
Castro and his crew of civilian heroes got back to
their ship in the Navy Yard. DeCastro changed
clothes. He was all but exhausted from more than
twenty-four hours of strenuous, nerve-racking work.
He was hungry, and eager to get home. A man in
overalls came up to him and held out a piece of paper:

"Hey, why didn't you fill out this overtime slip?"

DeCastro looked at him and all he could say
was, "Christamighty!"

Then, because buses could not operate in the blackout and because he had no other means of transportation, Julio DeCastro walked five miles through the darkened streets to his home.

IX

THE DEAD

Each afternoon for days the dead were buried. They died the deaths of heroes and were buried with the rites of the brave. They were buried simply and with dignity, without crowds of onlookers. The first were laid in the peace and quiet of Nuuanu Cemetery above the harbor where they fought. On each grave was placed a small bouquet of flowers—poinsettias, golden asters, and the many-colored island hibiscus. Golden sunlight spread out on the broad green lawn. Shadows lengthened fast, telling of the night.

An even row of tight-lipped, khaki-clad marines, their eyes fixed on the distant hills, stepped forward, raised their rifles, and fired three volleys over the graves of the glorious dead. A marine bugler sounded Taps. "Lights out. All quiet. Night has come." The clear notes of the bugle echoed through the quiet valley, a valley of legend and song, where happy people have lived in peace and freedom for over a hundred years.

A Catholic priest in black robes hallowed the ground with water. A Protestant chaplain blessed it with the committal ceremony. A Jewish chaplain added his blessings. No one else was there. No loved one knew. No mother, wife, or sister away on the mainland could come to them. Later, after the war is over, they will be lifted out again and buried in cemeteries in their own home towns. Until then they are here in a pleasant green valley, looking down upon the sea.

There have been burials every day since, most of them at the new Navy cemetery at Red Hill, called Halawa, until over two thousand American soldiers and sailors killed in the surprise attack have been laid to rest in Hawaiian soil.* Most of the services, like the first, have been unattended except for the marine firing squad and the chaplains. On New Year's Day Honolulu paid its respects to the dead in a memorial service at Nuuanu. Services were for almost four hundred sailors who lost their lives at Pearl Harbor and for three Hawaiian firemen who died at Hickam Field.

*See Chapter XIV: Historical Notes.

Several hundred persons attended, each wearing a flower lei in honor of the dead. They gathered around the ten long, wide trenches in which rows of men who had fought side by side now lay side by side, each in his own coffin. There was not a dry eye in the assembly as six Hawaiian girls sang the slow, sweet strains of "Aloha Oe"—"Until we meet again"— the saddest song ever sung at a funeral. The crowd stood with heads bare and bowed as a native Mormon missionary prayed.

Hawaiian women dressed in black, wearing leis of yellow feathers, laid long leis the full length of the graves. These were the Daughters of Hawaii, many of whom were descendants of warriors who fought and died long ago in this same valley.

Fleet Chaplain MacGuire spoke with respect and anger in his firm voice:

"Let no one think they died in vain. Our one hundred and thirty million Americans would glow if they had seen how our boys died.

"They manned their guns until the decks buckled under them from the heat. Not a whimper. Not a moan.

"It was glorious!"

"Don't say we buried our dead with sorrow. They died manfully. They were buried manfully. And we will avenge their deaths, come what may!" *

*See Chapter XIV: Historical Notes.

X

THE JAPANESE COMMUNITY

By the morning of the second day I was again able to view the Japanese in their true perspective, and I felt thoroughly ashamed of myself.

"I have lived in Hawaii since 1930," I thought. "Surely I can trust my judgment. Anyway, I don't have to trust it. Experts in the FBI and in the Army and Navy Intelligence services have told us not to get any foolish, hysterical ideas about the local Japanese."

Nevertheless, I wanted the latest word.

I found the palm-guarded Dillingham Building, home of the FBI, a chief center of interest. Onlookers were seated in the lobby, watching the round-up of supicious characters.

Three soldiers brought in a couple of Filipino boys. These prisoners were pretty harmless-looking specimens, tousle-headed, their shirt-tails sticking out, but the soldiers stalked them as cautiously as if the prisoners might pull out bombs and throw them at any minute. I thought the Filipinos had probably been guilty of violating the blackout last night. This is a serious offense, so serious in fact that the police have orders to shoot out lights if their first warnings are ignored. These Filipino lads may have been playing, but the FBI does not consider pranks in order just now.

Mr. Shivers stepped out of the elevator. He is a quiet, brown-eyed man from Ashland City, Tennessee, who does not live up to his name. There is neither detective glamour nor flatfoot crudeness about him. He would more readily be taken for a fashionable doctor than a man quick on the draw. Since December 7th, he has been co-ordinator of intelligence staffs in the Territory, and has been busy day and night directing the rounding-up of certain aliens and the questioning of suspects. I had a Coca-Cola with him at the Cafe Pierre next door, but saw that he was too busy to talk, and so did not attempt to ask him anything about the work. He remarked that Shunzo Sakamaki was with them now, that things certainly had happened fast, hadn't they?

I returned to the lobby to wait for Sakamaki, who,

until he joined the FBI, was a professor of political science and history at the University of Hawaii.

Sakamaki came in. He is the quiet, steady type of Japanese, the kind who make good surgeons. He has come into prominence as the president of the Oahu Citizens' Home Defense Committee, the most active committee of the Major Disaster Council, and one made up almost entirely of Japanese-Americans.

The Committee was just getting under way when Japan attacked. Its first official action was in response to the call for blood donors. Overnight they signed up more donors than had been obtained from all other racial groups in Honolulu combined.

Sixty key men from this group, of whom Sakamaki is one, are co-operating with the intelligence bureau of the Honolulu police, which has been trained by the FBI. These men are residents of different Japanese communities throughout the islands. They are not engaged in espionage work, but accept reports from any members of their districts who have reason to suspect sabotage. Many of the suspects who have been escorted into police headquarters were turned in by the Japanese community itself. Thus, by tapping the resources of Japanese loyalty, the three intelligence bureaus are doing a thorough job of sleuthing as well.

At no time since the war talk started years ago have we islanders thought that the Japanese in Hawaii would turn into a mass of saboteurs. We applauded when an Army spokesman a couple of years ago said that any idea of isolating the Japanese population by removing them all to one island had been abandoned. We have lived with them long enough to feel that they have the same ambitions, desires, and weaknesses that we have.

A great many mainland Americans believe that most of the Japanese in Hawaii are hiding in the sugarfields, ready at a signal to leap out and cut us down with their cane knives. The belief is the direct result of the many rumors which came with a whirlwind rush along with the blitz of December 7th. Most of these were spread over the mainland by a press correspondent who returned from Hawaii before checking his information with official sources.

"There was a powerful fifth column in Hawaii! The attacking Japs had minutely detailed information," it was said. "They knew just where each battleship was to berth. They bombed the useless old *Utah* mercilessly because the fine aircraft-carrier *Lexington* was scheduled to be there instead."

"A Hawaiian Japanese fifth columnist cut a broad

arrow in a canefield," it was said, "directing enemy pilots straight toward Pearl Harbor!"

"One of the Jap pilots shot down had on a McKinley High School ring."

"Japanese saboteurs stalled old jalopies across the road to Pearl Harbor, blocking traffic, holding up ambulances carrying the wounded, keeping officers and men from reaching their battle stations."

The FBI can give us the facts. Pearl Harbor has been exposed to public view for years. Anyone can drive along the public highway or take a hike over the hills behind the harbor and observe at leisure the navy's vital installations and warships. No doubt Japanese consular agents took these jaunts frequently. The navy protested against this situation, but Congress refused to pass legislation condemning property over-looking the harbor.

Admittedly, we do not know just how much information the attacking Japanese had. The truth is that, regardless of what advance knowledge they did have, they needed no fifth column to provide it. A general idea of whether ships were likely to be in the harbor was sufficient. A battleship is a huge object, visible for miles. It is about as difficult to make out as the Chrysler Building would be if it were lying on its side in the Hudson River. Once the Japanese knew where Pearl Harbor is—which any tourist map of Hawaii clearly shows—they did not need to know what berth each battleship normally took. The attackers struck at every battleship in the harbor, regardless of position, size, or age.

Corroborating evidence that the Japanese did not approach with the help and direction of fifth columnists has just come to light. The Japanese submarine which was sunk outside Pearl Harbor an hour or more before the attack has now been raised, and the ship's log has been translated. It tells how the submarine entered Pearl Harbor trailing a garbage scow, and cruised about, noting the types and numbers of warships inside. It then left and sent a radio message to the Japanese carriers, relaying the information.

The man cutting the arrow in the canefield was not needed, nor, as a matter of fact, was he there. He was an unconfirmed rumor.

Nor was any special information needed by the Japanese pilots in order to locate the hangars at Hickam Field. I do not know why these hangars were not built back in the mountainside, where they would be hidden from view. But there they lay, not only the biggest objects on all the island, but, furthermore, painted white and gleaming in the tropical sunlight. They were an invitation that the Japanese pilots could see for more than twenty miles.

The McKinley ring, like the cane-cutter, never materialized. A censor, whose business it was to run down rumor, told men he had checked with every official who had looked through the clothing and possessions of slain Japanese pilots. None had seen a McKinley ring.

If the local Japanese had blocked traffic on the three-lane highway to Pearl Harbor, they would have committed the most effective sabotage possible. This is the obvious kind of sabotage an organized group would commit. By disrupting the bedlam of traffic on December 7th, the Japanese could have cut the lifeline of island defense. However, officials found no indications of any such attempt.

Possibly the rumor that broke the back of all rumors in Hawaii concerned a canine saboteur. A woman excitedly telephoned the police station, "For the past three nights I've heard a dog barking in Japanese code! What shall I do?"

"Don't bother about the dog barking the signals," replied the policeman over the telephone. "Find the dog receiving them!"

I was told by the chief agent of the Federal Bureau of Investigation in Hawaii, "You can say without fear of contradiction that there has not been a single act of sabotage—either before December 7th, during the day of the attack, or at any time since."

Chief Gabrielson of the Honolulu police, who works in close collaboration with the Army, told me the same thing. "If the Japanese here had wanted to do damage, December 7th offered them a golden opportunity," he added.

"Where were the Japanese on that Sunday if they were not out sabotaging?"

"Hundreds of them were actively defending the Territory," the chief of police will tell you. "Many of them rushed to their posts as volunteer truck and ambulance drivers."

At Pearl Harbor, two Japanese boys saw a machine-gunner having some difficulty setting up his gun. They ran to him, helped him steady it for action, and fed him ammunition. Both worked so fast that they had to have emergency treatment for burns at the hospital.

When the call came over the radio for blood donors, again the Japanese were among the first to respond and by the hundreds. They stood in line at Queen's Hospital for hours, waiting to give their blood to save the lives of American soldiers.

A local Japanese-American boy was said to have

been on guard duty on the other side of the island when a Japanese officer from a damaged submarine climbed out and waded ashore. The local boy challenged the officer, first in English, then in Japanese, but got no reply. Then he stepped forward to the officer and slapped him.

"Do not strike me," the officer said, in good English. "I am a gentleman and expect to be treated as such."

"Gentleman, hell!" the sentry said. "You're one of those bastards that's responsible for me being out here on guard duty at twenty-one dollars a month!" And, smack! he slapped the officer again.

These loyal Americans of Japanese ancestry are on the spot. So far they have been remarkably level-headed. The strain on them is going to become even more intense as the weeks and months go on and the prospect of an attempted invasion of Oahu by the forces of Japan comes nearer. The pressure on them from Americans who distrust them will become greater. This pressure comes from the white man who says, "No matter what a Jap says, don't trust him. Once a Japanese, always a Japanese. Just let a Jap make one false move when I'm around!"

This man believes that skin color and race are more powerful than democracy. He is making it difficult for the intelligence forces in the islands to proceed on a basis of fact rather than on a basis of rumor and hysteria. According to the findings of the intelligence services, the fact is that not all Japanese are the same—that the second- and third-generation Japanese in Hawaii can be counted upon in any emergency, and that although the grandparent generation contains individuals who are sympathetic to the homeland in a nostalgic sort of way, they are not organized and the potentially dangerous have already been locked up.

The younger people have been grateful to their friends in Hawaii for not turning against them in this crisis. They were very thankful to Mr. Leslie Hicks, prominent Honolulu business man, when he gave a widely broadcast talk in favor of tolerance and fair treatment to the Japanese in Hawaii. He praised them for their fine record in the past and asked the American workers who arrived from the mainland recently to make a distinction between the Japanese imperialist government and the Japanese people living in Hawaii.

The Japanese in Hawaii have found the United States Army absolutely fair and impartial. At first there was a rumor that no Japanese would be taken into the army, and they were afraid that such official discrimination would foster all sorts of anti-Japanese feeling. They were relieved to find themselves drafted. "Now we have a chance to prove our loyalty," they said. They are convinced that they get a square deal in the army. On the day of the blitz a Japanese private, first class, rushed to his battle station, where he set such a good example of alertness and quick thinking that he was promoted to the rank of corporal the following week. This recognition reaffirmed the local Japanese belief in the fairness of the army.

One of the few ancient Japanese customs which has persisted during this conflict is that of giving the drafted youth of the family a farewell send-off to the wars. Ever so often, you see in one of the Japanese-language newspapers a little block advertisement, saying something like this:

Mr. and Mrs. K. Harada wish to thank all their friends who participated in last evening's celebration of the glorious induction of their eldest son, Kazuo, into the United States Army.

And they mean it. The Japanese believe that the son who works hard to become a good soldier will be appreciated by the authorities. They also believe that he will be promoted as fast as any white recruit, depending entirely upon his diligence and ability, regardless of his ancestry. They cannot help celebrating that.

The findings of the FBI and of the Army and Navy Intelligence services have agreed with the estimate of public opinion as to the loyalty of the Japanese in Hawaii. Of all the 425,000 people in the islands, only 273—and not all of them Japanese—have been detained as suspicious characters.

When Japanese aliens have been falsely suspected, they have taken the experience of detainment with philosophic understanding. One of these detainees who was subsequently released wrote the following charming letter to the commander of the camp:

I am very sure that all those detainees are fairly treated and all are satisfying at the camp. They are also willing to co-operate with you and warden and they are wishing to set example of good detainees so you can depend on them as much as co-operations are concern.

All are enjoying three good meals a day, but lack of vegetables and fruit and if it is permissible I do not mind to send papaias and bananas not every day but occasionally. I live in a country where many farmers and they are too glad to serve with their own products.

If I am allow to suggest a few things which I thought were good. Detainees want to read some things to keep up their moral and an English Gospel's such as St. John, St. Luke, St. Mark, and St. Matthew will enlighten them very much and also if checkers, cards, or indoor ball material for recreation will cheer them up very much and if it's permissionable, I am sure churches and Y.M.C.A. are too glad to send them in. . . .

In closing I wish to repeat thanks for your very good treatment while I was in the detention camp. Thank you again and again.

The authorities at the detention camp found it "permissionable" to follow his suggestions.

Everyone in Hawaii, Japanese as well as the rest of us, felt relieved and gratified when it was officially announced that not a single act of sabotage had been committed in Hawaii since the war began. The "new methods" initiated two years ago by Chief Agent Shivers seemed to be working. The authorities are taking no chances, but neither are they terrorizing the population.

"How long do you think your method would last in Japan?" a skeptic asked Mr. Shivers.

"This is not Japan," he replied.*

*See Chapter XIV: Historical Notes.

XI

THE NIIHAU STORY

EVERYONE IN HAWAII WAS THRILLED AND DELIGHTED with "the Niihau story," as it was immediately called. We were delighted because the irrepressible Hawaiians had not failed us. When it comes down to the fundamentals of manhood and womanhood—the good old eternal virtues of courage and loyalty—the Hawaiians are right there, fighting with the rest. It pleased us, too, because it localized World War II, made it Hawaii's war, to a degree at least. Dogfights have taken place above battlefields the world over, but "the Niihau story," with all its circumstances of locality and Hawaiian character, could never have occurred anywhere else.

The Niihau islanders have always known peace. The present owner, whom the Hawaiians regard as a benevolent "chief," is Mr. Aylmer Robinson. His island is only one hundred and twenty miles from metropolitan Honolulu, yet it might as well be one hundred and twenty thousand for all the modernizations that have come to its people. This story began soon after the attack on December 7th. Honolulu papers did not get it until December 16th. On Niihau they have no telephones, no radios, no electric lights, no automobiles. No whiskey has been allowed on the island in more than sixty years. Tobacco is prohibited. For generations, the little group of Hawaiians on Niihau have quietly tended their sheep and cattle, unmindful of the cares of the rest of the world. Yet when America was attacked, this most remote and tranquil of all her communities was brought into the battle on the very first day.

The villagers of Puuwai, the only inhabited spot on the island, were just arriving at their little church for worship when they were surprised to see two airplanes circling overhead, one of them sputtering and smoking badly.

"*Pilikia! Pilikia!*" ("Trouble! Trouble!") shouted one of the cowboys.

The planes banked and hovered over the village.

"Look! Red spots on the wings! The Rising Sun!

Not American—Japanese plane!" cried a quick-eyed Hawaiian boy.

The planes winged out to sea. The group of Hawaiians entered the church door, exchanging excited speculations. The cowboy-preacher complained of an inattentive congregation.

It was about two o'clock in the afternoon when one of the bombers returned, roaring in circles above the quiet village.* The island watched the pilot attempt a landing on a slope nearby and crash about seventy-five feet from the house of one of the husky cowboys, Hawila Kaleohano.

Hawila ran out to the craft. Pulling open the cabin door, he saw a helmeted Japanese pilot reaching for a revolver. The big Hawaiian cowboy moved like tropic lightning. He grabbed the gun and wrenched the Japanese out of the plane with such force that he snapped the heavy leather safety belt that harnessed the pilot to his seat. Even before the dazed Japanese picked himself up, he began to fumble inside his shirt as if searching for something. This was plain speaking to Hawila, who immediately tore open the pilot's shirt and commandeered a small bundle of maps and papers.

The Japanese had landed, but Hawila had the situa-

*See Chapter XIV: Historical Notes.

tion well in hand. Hawila didn't know there was a war on, but he did not wait for a formal declaration.

Villagers clustered about the plane. All of Niihau's one hundred and eighty inhabitants talked at once. They pointed to the bullet holes in the plane, darting questions at Hawila and his captive. What was the Japanese doing here? Was there a war? Had he been in a fight? Had Honolulu been attacked? How did he get those holes in his plane? What happened to the plane they had seen earlier in the day, smoking and sputtering? To all these questions, the pilot shook his head is if to say, "No speak English," although it later developed that he not only understood it, but spoke it fluently. All during the questioning, the Japanese had agitatedly attempted to snatch back the papers which Hawila had taken from him.

Had Niihau been equipped with wireless or telephone—if a single person on the island had owned even a small radio receiving set—the Hawaiians would have known that at that very moment Pearl Harbor was in flames, Hickam Field was a shambles, Kaneohe Naval Air Base practically destroyed, and that this man in their midst was a dangerous enemy. But not knowing these things, they were eager to hear the pilot tell his story. They sent to Kie-kie for Harada, the Japanese beekeeper, to act as interpreter.

Harada, who took a leading role in the events to follow, was a newcomer to Niihau, having been there for only a year.

Questioning was resumed through the interpreter, but the pilot refused to explain the bullet holes in the plane, and would not admit that there had been an attack on Honolulu. He demanded that Hawila return the "war-papers," as the Hawaiians were now referring to them; but Hawila, a staunch steward, kept them, intending to turn them over intact to his "chief," Mr. Robinson, who was on Kauai, an island 15 miles away.

Fortunately, Mr. Robinson was to return the next day when the weekly sampan brought provisions from Kauai; so the invader was put in a house, fed and guarded through the night, awaiting custody of Mr. Robinson.

The next day, after a brisk early morning ride, a group of Hawaiian cowboys, escorting the Japanese prisoner, pulled in their mounts at Kii landing. Shading their eyes with their hands, they peered anxiously out across the blue Pacific towards Kauai, searching the sea for the little sampan which should be riding at the wharf.

"*Pilikia*," one of them muttered. "Mr. Robinson never late."

Noon came, but still no sampan appeared. They waited until darkness fell; then reluctantly turned their mounts homeward.

On Tuesday, the Hawaiians again took the 15-mile ride to Kii with their prisoner, waited in vain, and again at dusk rode home in moody silence.

By Wednesday, they were saying, "Kauai also is in trouble. Maybe on all the islands there is great *pilikia*."

It was on Thursday that Harada, who, as one of the pilot's guards had been in constant conversation with the enemy for four days, sought out the four Hawaiian leaders.

"To keep the prisoner here in Puuwai village is bad," he said, "make much trouble. The women and children are afraid to leave their homes. The men sit here on the porch and talk of *pilikia*, and do no work. Why not take the pilot to my house at Kie-kie? It is quiet there."

"*Mai-kai*—good," said the unsuspecting Hawaiians; and they placed the enemy in Harada's custody, assigning Hawaiian guards to accompany them the two miles to Kie-kie.

The only other resident at Kie-kie was another Japanese, named Shintani. He was the head bee-keeper, an old man who had lived on Niihau for many years. He had married a Niihau woman, and together they had reared a family of Hawaiian-Japanese children. Now, Harada dismissed the Hawaiian guards and called in Shintani. The officer wished to speak with his two countrymen.

What the pilot said to these two men, we do not know. Possibly he spoke to them in nostalgic terms of Japan, and of their everlasting allegiance to the God-Emperor who forever required them to do their duty no matter how far they were from snow-capped Fujiyama and the green isles of the homeland. Perhaps he threatened to kill them if they did not do as he, the Samurai, ordered. In any event, he was successfully persuasive; and before the trio went to sleep their plans were laid.

Early the next morning, the cowboy Hawila was pulling on his *palaka* shirt when Shintani appeared in the doorway of his home. Could he please have the maps and papers which Hawila was safe-keeping for the honorable pilot who was now well and would like to have them back?

"No!" said Hawila.

Well, then, since Hawila would not return the papers, the honorable pilot would be willing to pay handsomely for the simple favor of having them burned. Shintani displayed $200 in United States currency—more money than Hawila had ever dreamed of seeing in his life.

"*Hua-kele!*" (Get out—fast!)

That was the last seen of Shintani. Afraid to return with an unfavorable report, the old Japanese fled to the woods.

Precisely why the Japanese pilot set such a high value upon the papers we do not know. Apparently, he did not want possession of them for himself so much as he wished to keep them from falling into enemy hands. The maps may have given the positions of the Japanese aircraft carriers from which Pearl Harbor had been bombed. Among the papers may have been the code by which to decipher Japanese radio messages. Perhaps a future military campaign was outlined there. If the blood of a true Samurai coursed through this Japanese officer's veins, he would be eager to die rather than allow such vital information to fall into the hands of the enemy. Possibly, however, he was not a high-souled Samurai at all, but was thinking only of saving his skin. What if these papers held proof that he was a spy? As a prisoner of war, he would be subject to mere imprisonment; but if the papers showed him to be a spy, he would be shot.

Whatever his reasons, he was determined to get those papers. He had only begun to fight back.

When after a reasonable length of time Shintani had failed to return, the pilot and Harada put their part of the plan into action. They were in the honey-house, where Harada was working and to which an unarmed Hawaiian guard named Hana-kai had agree-bly brought the prisoner so that the two Japanese could converse. Apparently the hospitable Hawaiians could not resist treating even a Japanese prisoner as a guest.

"I have finished here," Harada announced; "I now have important task at warehouse."

The two Japanese led the way to the warehouse, Hana-kai following. The moment they were inside the door, the pilot seized a shotgun which Harada had planted for him. His accomplice whipped out a revolver, and they backed the astonished Hawaiian to the wall.

"One cry-out and I kill you!" hissed Harada. Then the two Japanese cautiously withdrew from the ware-house, bolting the door behind them.

Now began the second phase of "The Battle of Niihau." Harada and the pilot headed at once for the village—and the bombing plane's machine guns. On the road, was a crowd of hapless Hawaiian joyriders. A Hawaiian woman and her seven children, decked in flower *leis*, were riding in a horse-drawn buggy. Perched in carefree Niihau style astride the horse was a long-legged Hawaiian girl.

Here was quick transportation to the village. The pilot grabbed the horse's reins and gave orders to Harada in Japanese. The assistant translated into English.

"Get out, quick!" he commanded the family in the buggy. To the girl on horseback he said, "Not you. Stay where you are!"

Pushing and shoving the frightened woman and children as they climbed out of the buggy, Harada forced them to line up, one behind another, and held his shotgun to the back of the little girl at the end of the row.

"No move! Anybody move, everybody die, one bullet!" he threatened.

The two Japanese leaped into the buggy. Pointing his shotgun at the brown-legged girl on the horse, Harada commanded:

"Turn around. Go Hawila's house! Hurry!" They were off towards the village at a gallop, the young girl sitting straight on the bareback horse, her black hair flying. Each Japanese clung to one arm of the jolting buggy with his free hand, and clutched his gun with the other.

"Stop now," ordered Harada just before they reached Hawila's house at the entrance to the village. The two Japanese descended from the buggy and approached on foot, hoping to surprise Hawila. But Hawila, forewarned by Shintani's attempted bribe, was on the alert. Seeing the two armed Japanese coming in the front gate, he calmly exited through the back door. As he leaped over the cereus-covered lava wall that enclosed his yard, he was joined by the guard Hana-kai, who had escaped from the warehouse. Hana-kai had climbed into the warehouse loft, jumped out a window twenty feet above the ground, and raced the Japanese to Puuwai. Together, the two Hawaiians hastened to the house where the cowboys usually gathered before riding out to work. Several were there, and they held a hasty council of war. Kekuhina, one of the men who was in charge during Mr. Robinson's absence, said,

"We have no choice. The great signal fire that lies always ready on the cliffs looking toward Kauai must be lighted. Since the days of the ancients, it has summoned the men of Kauai when disaster has threatened Niihau."

Hawila, Hana-kai, and four others set out through the woods to light the pyre.

Harada and the pilot ransacked Hawila's house, but could not find the papers. Enraged, the pilot strode out to the disabled plane, hauled out its two machine guns and full ammunition, set them up in a carriage, trained them on the village, and started firing. Bullets tore straight through the little frame houses. Windows shattered, shingles popped off porch roofs, cactus splinters whizzed through the air. The villagers, all of whom were hearing the staccato report of machine-gun fire for the first time in their lives, fled out their back doors. Shielding themselves behind fences and running to the cover of tall grass and cactus, some sought the woods and some the caves along the sea-shore.

When the Japanese judged that the entire popula-tion was terrorized, they took their guns and marched through the village. As they went from house to house, Harada called out:

"Where is Hawila? Tell us where Hawila is or we shoot!"

They found the village deserted except for old Mrs. Hulu-o-ulani, who had stolidly refused to flee with the others. She was sitting quietly in a rocking chair, read-ing her Bible, when the Japanese burst in.

"Where has Hawila gone?" demanded Harada.

"I know, but I will not tell you," she answered calmly.

"Listen, old one! You will tell us where Hawila lies hidden, or we will kill you!" Harada threatened.

"Only God has power over life and death," Mrs. Hulu-o-ulani said sternly, "and anyone else who interferes with it will be punished."

The two Japanese looked at each other blankly. They turned to the door and walked out.

The desperate pair began their search all over again, making a frantic house-to-house scrutiny for the papers.

At dusk, Hawila and his men returned from the signal fire to the cactus woods on the outskirts of the village where most of the people were gathered. There, while one man kept watch, they huddled together in a final council of war. It was decided that all the women and children should hide in caves for the night and that Hawila with five strong men should row across the 15-mile channel to Kauai and bring back aid. The other men would keep watch on the Japanese and try to capture them.

But they had another duty first. Before any start was made, the Hawaiians wished to ask divine guidance in their undertakings. They waited until the

Japanese entered a house at the far side of the village. Then, in the falling dusk, the men crept quietly to the little church, went inside, knelt on the rough floor, and prayed to God.

The Japanese continued their feverish search, not even stopping to eat. They were getting nearer now to the stables where Niihau's famous breed of Arabian horses were quartered. Hawila and his men had to reach these stables to get mounts to take them to the emergency whaleboat at Kii, fifteen miles away. Just as the six men stealthily approached the stables, a horse neighed loudly. Warned, the Japanese headed for the stables, shooting as they ran. The Hawaiians dashed into the stalls and charged out again on horseback. Harada blasted with both barrels. The pilot opened up with his machine-gun. But the Hawaiian cowboys, lying low on their bareback mounts, scattered in all directions and melted into the darkness. Not one was hit.

They rode pell-mell down the village path, followed the west shoreline ten miles, galloped across the grassy pasture lands to Kii on the east coast. They jumped into the heavy whaleboat, seized the oars, and pushed out upon the rough channel for Kauai.

But developments on Niihau did not wait for the rescue partly to return with aid from Kauai.

In the village, the final phase of the miniature campaign was racing swiftly to a dramatic conclusion. The Japanese had captured one of the Hawaiians who had been watching their operations from ambush. They tied his hands behind his back and naïvely dispatched him to Kie-kie with a message to Harada's wife. He started off obediently; but as soon as he was out of sight of the Japanese, he turned back to the cactus woods. There he searched out the native who was to play the stellar role in the epic's ending—Beni-hakaka Kana-hele.

Kana-hele had long been a leader among the Niihau people. He was wise with years, and powerful in body. He could carry three one-hundred-and-thirty-pound cases of honey at a time; he could grab an attacking wild boar by the ears, throw him, and finish him off with a knife; he had often slipped into a quiet bay where sharks slept in shallow water, leaped onto a shark's back and had the thrill of a fast ride for as long as he could hold on to the frightened demon of the sea.

Kana-hele and his partner decided to raid the enemy's base of supplies. Under cover of darkness, while the Japanese were again searching Hawila's house, the Hawaiians inched their way up the village street, seized the entire cache of ammunition, and lugged it deep into the woods.

Ransacking Hawila's house this time with a vengeance, the Japanese uncovered the pilot's map and revolver; but even tearing up floor planks and destroying attic walls failed to reveal the "war-papers." Hawila had hidden the papers in a secret place where he knew the natives would look for them if he were killed, but which no outsider would ever find. Such a hiding place is customary in every Hawaiian community; it is never disclosed to other races, not even when they are inter-married with the Hawaiians.

The failure of their search infuriated the Japanese. Just before dawn, in a last desperate gesture, they set fire to Hawila's house and burned it to the ground, doubtless hoping that the papers might burn with it. Then they sprinkled the plane with gasoline and burned it also, perhaps to prevent its eventual salvage by Americans. They may have planned to escape from the island. Perhaps the best guess is that having recovered the pilot's maps, they hoped to capture the motor-sampan when it arrived with Mr. Robinson. With luck, they might reach the Carolines in it. Before leaving, however, they must find Hawila, and force him at the point of a gun to reveal the hiding place of the papers.

But between them and success in these two ventures, lay the courage of one man and one woman.

Beni-hakaka Kana-hele had taken his family to the beach to spend the night. Now, at dawn, he and his wife were returning to the outskirts of the village. Suddenly they were confronted by the pilot and Harada, and were looking into the barrels of a shotgun and a revolver.

"We want Hawila," Harada said. "You, Kana-hele, know the many paths in the woods. You know where Hawila hides. Take us to him."

Kana-hele knew that Hawila had rowed with the rescue party to Kauai, but he pretended to search for him. He led the Japanese behind the village, through the cactus thicket, and into the woods. His wife followed.

"Hawila! Hawila!" Kana-hele's deep, strong voice echoed through the woods. He led the party along a cow trail that ran between high cactus plants and *Koa* trees, ending by a wall made of jagged lava rock.

The pilot realized he was being duped. His brown face turned red. Sweat stood out on his forehead. He yelled in rage to Harada. Harada shouted angrily at Kana-hele and his wife:

"He will shoot you! Shoot everybody if you no find Hawila!"

The pilot did not want to shoot Kana-hele and his wife; he wanted them to lead him to Hawila. His shotgun was already loaded; but in order to frighten the Hawaiian couple, he said to Harada in English:

"Hand me two cartridges. One for the man. One for the woman."

Harada took two cartridges from the box and handed them to the pilot. As their hands met, the 6-foot Hawaiian jumped the Japanese flier. The shotgun fell from the pilot's hands, but Harada grabbed it.

For a moment the pilot and Kana-hele rocked back and forth. Then the Japanese got his arm free and jerked his pistol from his boot, where he had hidden it. He attempted to pull the trigger; but Kana-hele's wife, following the example of Hawaiian women of old who went into battle with their men, dove for his arm and caught it before he could fire.

At a command from the pilot, Harada stepped into the fray and grappled with the powerful woman.

"Hua-kele!——Get away!" Kana-hele shouted to Harada. "Do not touch my wife. If you hurt her, I will kill you when I am finished here."

Harada ignored the warning, succeeded in pulling the wife away and threatened to kill her.

The pilot, his revolver-arm free, shot Kana-hele.

The bullet went into his stomach. The wounded Hawaiian rushed the Japanese again. The pilot shot him again, in the thigh. He shot him a third time, in the groin.

"Then," Kana-hele later told the American interpreter who took down his story, "I got mad!"

The enraged Hawaiian came down upon the Japanese like a killer whale upon a shark. He grabbed him up by his leg and neck as he would have a sheep, swung him around in the air, and hurled him with terrific force against the lava stone wall.

Then Kana-hele turned to keep his promise to Harada. He was not needed there. The stocky Japanese was clumsily placing the muzzle of the long shotgun against his own stomach, attempting to commit hara-kiri. He was in such a hurry that he missed, as the shotgun kicked itself out of his hands. He grabbed it up and aimed it at himself again. This time he succeeded, emptied both barrels into his stomach.

Kana-hele turned quickly to the pilot. He was not needed there, either. The Hawaiian's wife had again rushed to his aid, this time armed with a rock.

"She was plenty *hu-hu*, [angry], that woman," Kana-hele told the interpreter. "She started right in to beat that pilot's brains out. She did a pretty good job."

By this time, Beni-hakaka Kana-hele, with three bullets in his middle, wasn't feeling so well. He sat down by the bloody stone wall. His wife ran to the village for help. But while aid was coming on horseback, Kana-hele got tired of waiting, got up, and walked to the village alone.

Hawila returned from Kauai with a squad of men from the 299th Infantry; but they were not needed, except to round up Shintani and Harada's wife for the concentration camp.

So ended the Battle of Niihau. The Japanese invader was the first armed enemy to assume command over free Americans on their own soil in more than 150 years. Fully equipped with modern weapons, he was overcome by two Hawaiians, unarmed except with native strength and courage and the primitive rocks of their own island.

When Major General Rapp Brush pinned American Legion hero medals on Hawila and Kana-hele, he said: "You showed fine qualities. When put upon, you took the only action decent people could take."

In Honolulu, we said: "Warn the Japanese not to shoot Hawaiians more than twice. The third time, they get mad!" *

---

*See Chapter XIV: Historical Notes.

XII

A YEAR AFTER

AFTER THE FIRST WEEK OF THE WAR, I THOUGHT THAT if you were to visit Hawaii for the first time, or even return after a long absence, you would not at once find it remarkably different from what you expected. More things are unchanged than changed. The contour of the island is the same. The glorious heights are still here, and the deep valleys. All the landmarks you look for from the ship—Diamond Head, the clouds above Tantalus, the light showers turning the upper valleys purple, the welcoming green foliage— all these, even down to Aloha Tower and the big pineapple-shaped water tank high above the cannery, are the same.

As you walk from the boat up Bishop Street, you see the changes that the war has made in Hawaii's daily life and habits. You would miss the *lei*-sellers who used to line the docks, holding out fragrant armloads of brilliant *ilima*, *pikake*, and ginger flowers to the delight of tourist and *kamaaina* alike. War put an end to Honolulu's most colorful industry, and the handsome *lei*-women are "somewhere on Oahu" busily making camouflage nets to hide the army's gun emplacements from possible enemy raiders. Their skillful fingers, instead of stringing vari-colored flowers, are weaving vari-colored bits of cloth onto fish net bases according to blueprint patterns supplied by the U. S. Army Engineers.

In place of the *lei*-sellers, you would see women in the grey uniforms of the Motor Corps stepping into banana wagons; men in khaki, rifles in hand, on guard in front of the newspaper buildings, radio stations, and power plants; nuns, robed and hooded, wearing their gas-masks suspended beside their rosaries; children carrying their special "bunny masks" as they go to their trench-equipped schools.

When you look through the rental advertisements for a place to stay, you may be attracted to "Kalihi— out of evacuation area. Airy room with blackout and bomb shelter." And, if this is not sufficiently reassuring, you will find in the "Miscellaneous for Sale" column adjoining, "Sand Bags. Will Deliver."

We old-timers claim that Waikiki, the tourist haven, has improved. It is not crowded. You will have to step carefully to avoid barricades of barbed wire on your way to the water, but it is the same as it has been for years—once you are in.

Usually I swim from Gray's out to the raft a couple of hundred yards away, then down to Fort DeRussy. The other day, as I swam to within ten or fifteen strokes of the raft, I saw a fence of barbed wire stretching from the raft to one part of the shore, keeping the Fort free and the channel clear of visitors. You are glad to know that the Army is taking no chances.

If you know Honolulu well, you will soon discover the other changes. One of the most striking is that of Punahou School, long famed as "the oldest school west of the Rockies." Its boast is that in the rough 'Forties and 'Fifties of the past century, residents of Oregon and California used to send their children to Punahou rather than allow them to brave the trip across country to go to school in the East. Punahou celebrated its double-golden anniversary just last June. Before it was well started on its hundred and first year, the war struck.

The first night U. S. Engineers moved into the spacious grounds, took over the buildings, and began working fast. Several of the girls and teachers living in the dormitory woke up Monday morning to find themselves reclining in an army canteen. A few teachers, stayed on, ladling out soup to hungry workers.

The detail of the campus which has weathered the change best is the stone wall, made of lava-rock and covered with a vigorous hedge of night-blooming cereus. The jagged rock and the prickly cactus plant match the mood of bayonets and barbed wire very well. Townspeople have always come out at night in droves when the hundred-year-old cereus hedge blossoms. It is probably the most gorgeous of its kind in the world, stretching for over a mile, and throwing thousands of golden centered white lanterns open to the moon. When it blooms again, it will be for the eyes of the U. S. Engineers alone. Nobody travels at night, and by day the flowers are wilted. . . . And the Engineers will not have time to look at them.

The University, under the direction of its new president, Professor Gregg M. Sinclair, is the only American university operating in a war area. Its broad green, palm-shaded campus is zig-zagged with trenches. Professors and girls—there are relatively few boys, most of the former students now being in either defense work or in military service—grab their gas masks and leap into the trenches and bomb shelters when the air raid warning siren sounds.

President Sinclair, a man of tremendous enthusiasm and broad vision, has revamped the curriculum in Economics to show the causes of aggression, in Mathematics to give technical training to engineers and navigators, in History to interpret the world conflict, and in studies of American culture to emphasize the democratic traditions on which our nation stands.

University people have worked full time and overtime ever since December 7th. Language experts are helping the Army censors and the various intelligence services. Even before the attack, Naval Intelligence had snatched Dr. Denzel Carr, who speaks thirty languages and reads more than fifty. Biologists and chemists are continuously taking samples of water from different parts of town, testing them for poison or harmful bacteria. Dr. Allen says people hear that tests are being made and immediately find something wrong with their water. "It tastes funny," they claim, until it is proved pure. Dr. Allen is quite reassuring. He says the Japanese would have to pour a ship-load of arsenic into our water supply before they could poison the population.

One out of every fifteen islanders is an air raid warden, an auxiliary policeman, or other worker in active civilian defense. Gordon Smith and John Black, our Tantalus neighbors, are members of the Business Men's Training Corps. They have drilled, patrolled, and had target practice, making themselves part of an efficient regiment ready for active duty if the island is invaded. I had been up Tantalus with Gordon shooting at tin cans, but he never thought that the practice with his Sears-Roebuck gun would stand him in good stead on the rifle range.

Our people of all races and color stand in line to buy war bonds until every bond counter in town, from the Bank of Hawaii to the Moana Hotel, runs out of issuing blanks. Our first campaign quota was a million dollars worth—we bought nine million.

Everyone is doing something, even if it is only being immunized against typhoid, smallpox, and diphtheria. If the Japanese try a germ-borne invasion, we will be prepared, and if not, at least we have guaranteed ourselves against war-time epidemics. Hawaii is the first civilian community to be completely inoculated against disease in this war.

Of course, you would miss regular mail. Now that we have convoys, we never know when mail is coming or going, and occasionally there are long lapses between deliveries. If you are eager to hear from people you love, you may be unnecessarily upset.

Fortunately, you can still send a wire and even telephone. Censors are everywhere, but they are interested in suppressing only information that might be helpful to the enemy.

I talked to my wife in New York, and it was the best thirteen dollars I ever spent. I had been warned not to mention any names of persons, places, or ships, the weather, any movement of troops or numbers of planes. I had no such information. Even so I broke the rules three or four times before I knew it—the first thing I said was "Ruby!" It was a name, and so tabu, but it is hard to talk to your wife without mentioning her name.

The story is told of a newly wed army wife whose husband was on emergency duty and did not get home for a week. She rang him up every day. The fifth day she said, "I don't care if that old thing *is* listening in, I'm going to tell you I still love you!"

Mr. Frear read in the paper one morning an Army order to the effect that every man on the island would be expected to procure his own tools and build an air-raid shelter, large enough to protect himself and the members of his family. We immediately got to work. I suggested the location—that is, I said I thought it ought to be in the back yard rather than the front. Mr. and Mrs. Frear selected the exact location under a *kiawe* tree near the sundial where Ruby and I were married. They furnished the tools. All Yamato had to do was throw out several tons of dirt. The result is a trench, seven feet deep, two and a half or three feet wide, and forty feet long, and we are very proud of it.

It has a zig, a zag, and a zig. We enter at either zig and stand in the covered zag. The theory is that if shrapnel enters either zig it will fly into the dirt wall and not reach us. Yamato has planted tomatoes in the pile of fresh dirt around the shelter and on top of the zag.

The shelter was first used a few weeks after the blitz. A long alarm was sounded from Aloha Tower and from other warning signals recently installed in the various sections of town. Some of the Punahou girls who were having classes here at the house, ran gleefully into it. Unfortunately I could not join them. I was in a bus on the way to Kaneohe, and the bus-man did not stop. A series of short blasts told us the alert was over. It was announced later that somebody got the signals crossed and sounded the long alarm for the beginning, when it should have been the short. Since then, short blasts announce the alarm, a long one ends it.

If you have friends in Hawaii and want to send

them something they will like, send a map and a flashlight with some extra batteries. All the maps in town were sold out the day after the war started. Some of us here hardly knew where the fighting was. We heard Kuala Lumpur mentioned on the radio, and it sounded bad for the British, but that's about all we understood.

The flashlight, of course, is for use while we wander about in the parts of the house not blacked out. I have been surprised to learn how badly I can get turned around in a place where I have lived for months at a time. I always thought there were fourteen steps leading up to my bedroom, but the first night I stumbled on the fifteenth and then again on the sixteenth. Try putting toothpaste on your toothbrush in the dark. And taking a bath! A fellow at Kaneohe said he had great difficulty because he lost the soap in the bathtub, but that he was getting along all right now since he had bought some black soap!

It takes about twice as long to make up a bed in the dark as in the daylight. I have found that the easiest way is to get in bed first. Pull the sheet up and smooth it out to each side of the bed. Then the first blanket, then the second. If the sheet needs to be tucked in at the bottom, turn on the—"For God's sake, put out that light before the policeman shoots it out!"

Some unlucky persons have not yet blacked out any room in the house, so that they have to eat early and then sit around in complete darkness. Even so, they are not much worse off than those who have not figured out some kind of scheme for ventilating the room that is blacked out. One way to do it is to make a zig-zag entrance and leave the door open.

I feel guilty whenever I tell anybody here about our luxurious blackout room. It's air conditioned. The three of us sit here in perfect comfort, turning the indicator up or down as we wish to change the temperature of the room. I sit here at the typewriter, Mrs. Frear knits for the Red Cross, at the same time reading from a book on a stand set up in front of her, and Mr. Frear works busily revising his account of Hawaii in the Encyclopaedia Britannica so that the new edition will include the attack on Pearl Harbor.

We all knock off for the news. At seven o'clock Mr. Frear bends over close to the radio and listens to every word Jim Wahl says on the Shell News program, again for Bill Norwood at 7:30, and once more for the CBS round-the-world news. If a man's voice continues on the radio directly after the news is over, Mr. Frear listens intently to catch any late bulletin. Frequently he bends his ear close and hears "Buy the tonic that will give you hair that men, and especially women, admire." He raises his heavy gray eyebrows, smiles, and shakes his head as if to say, "I don't need any of that!"

People in Hawaii would feel ashamed if you thought that we take the war lightly. We joke about the blackout and the gasoline restrictions, but we are also proud of General Delos C. Emmon's statement that our blackout is more successful than London's. If we laugh, it is because we know that compared to the sacrifices made by our soldiers and sailors, our civilian sacrifices are trivial.

Honolulu morale is high. We have learned that our civilian morale is the result of our preparedness. We see that morale depends upon what goes on before war strikes. The Hawaii Medical Association is treasuring a telegram from George Baehr, M.D., Chief Medical Officer for Civilian Defense in Washington. It reads:

Territorial Medical Association: Office of Civilian Defense requests you urge all hospitals to establish immediately emergency medical field units in accord with plan outlined in Medical division bulletin Nos. 1 and 2 and drill weekly. When necessary, reserve field unit should be organized with Medical G. W. nursing and training volunteer personnel derived from the community. Urge immediate action.

This telegram arrived just two and one-half days after twenty such units had been in action. To appreciate the preparation it takes to train a complete medical unit, you must know that a single unit consists of two doctors, two dentists, eight nurses, eight surgical aides, eight supply men, one supply clerk, six stenographers, nine utility men, sixty-four litter bearers, two dietitians, two motorcyclists, two messengers, six ambulance drivers, and three ambulances—one hundred and twenty persons in all. When you remember that the Hawaii Medical Association had *twenty* units, a total of two thousand four hundred persons, in the field on the morning of the bombing, you see what a deal of preparation the doctors had made.

Many of the two thousand four hundred persons who sprang to activity on that December Sunday had received eighty-two hours of instruction. For months busy doctors voluntarily met groups of people in hot schoolrooms after work at night. It was boresome, tiring labor. They had "dry-runs," rehearsing an emergency, pushing ambulances out, carrying each other around on stretchers, and wrapping each other up in bandages. All this shadow-play seemed foolish to people looking on from the outside who did not think there was going to be any emergency anyway.

But on December 7th, their preparation gave spirit to the rest of us, and, in many cases, an outlet to our own energies. The marvelous expression of public desire to help by contributing blood could not have happened had Dr. Pinkerton and others not already had the blood bank in working order. Doctors who worked at Pearl Harbor and Tripler Hospital do not like to think what those first six hours would have been like without the plasma that was already in the bank and that was rushed to them by Dr. Pinkerton. They are mighty glad that the far-sighted Doctor pushed the idea of a blood bank months and months ago. Some persons had thought he was a scare-monger.

"A thousand flasks of blood plasma! What did the man think was going to happen? A war?" The Doctor did not get his thousand flasks, but the two hundred and ten he did get proved to be such a godsend that they inspired the whole community.

Social life in Honolulu is both limited and intimate. Most of the time you stay at home in your blacked out room. When you visit friends in the evening, you go prepared to spend the night. The consequences of getting caught out after curfew are too serious to risk. Hawaii is under martial law, and people who move about at night without authorization have some tall explaining to do when they face the provost court.*

The provost marshal is a figure of whom we are very much aware in Hawaii. The reason is not so much that we see more police on the streets as that the provost marshal makes good newspaper copy, and has caught on with the public—although not always with the local lawyers. There have been several marshals, but Lt. Col. Neal D. Franklin, a big, blackhaired, six-footer, brought informality into the court and human interest stories into the public press.

Colonel Franklin is tough. Collections of fines at the Honolulu jail alone for the first six months from December to June were nearly sixty thousand dollars, skyrocketed from two thousand dollars for the same period of the previous year. The daily average has been about one hundred cases, bringing collections of fifteen hundred dollars. Blackout violations lead all the rest. "Black out at home, or blackout in jail" is the court's motto. First offenders usually draw a five dollar fine, and spend ten days in jail if they come back again. One man showed up for a third time. Police officers claimed that he had a habit of leaving his lights on until the police beat on the door.

*See Chapter XIV: Historical Notes.

He then shut them off quickly, jumped into bed, and insisted that the lights were not on in the first place. Colonel Franklin gave him thirty days.

A Pearl Harbor taxi driver with a long record for speeding was brought before the provost marshal. "A clear case of high blood pressure. You'd better give some of it away," advised the Colonel. The blood bank at Queen's Hospital has a line of donors from court almost every day.

Honolulu people, reading the writeups of the provost marshal's day, have found him to be fair and impartial. A young Navy officer heard from him on the subject of speeding: "The only speeding I will permit you to do is to catch up with and destroy enemy airplanes or submarines," he declared. Not long afterwards he rebuked two army officers for the same offense. "In the service, you are supposed to set an example in driving your car. I can conceive of no excuse for traveling at that rate except possibly to save life, which was not the case with you."

Occasionally the marshal runs into island and Oriental superstition. A Chinese woman, brought in for blackout violation, pleaded that the light in her room was turned on by a ghost after she had retired. "Well," said the Colonel, "I will not doubt the word of a lady, but I suggest that after this you remove the bulb and if the ghost returns, notify the police immediately!"

A Filipino, guilty of a minor violation, was ordered to buy a bond. A few days later he reported to the court, proudly displaying a certificate marked "Bomber for Bataan." The Filipino understood the judge to say "Buy a bomber," so he had contributed thirty-seven fifty to a current campaign.

A Hawaiian, guilty of wife-beating—a pastime which has been on the increase since the blackout, was ordered to do the family washing for thirty days or spend the time in jail. A Chinese man, indulging in the same pleasure, was sentenced to sixty days, but told to continue his job as a defense worker in the daytime. Instead of going home at night, however, he goes to jail until his sentence has been served.

Perhaps the most unusual case to come before the provost court was tried in rural Oahu before Marshal Major Henry DuPree. The Major ordered eighteen alien Japanese to pay a total of eight hundred and seventy-five dollars in fines to the United States defense fund. They had stolen fifty dollars' worth of lumber from a defense project to build bomb shelters to protect themselves from their own countrymen!

The police, like the court, are very busy, but only with minor violations. Crime in Hawaii disappeared with the lights of the city. The long dark hours have brought back the *Kahuna*—Hawaiian witchcraft—however, to some sections, or so we would believe from a story which delighted *Star Bulletin* readers.

At 1:25 A.M., the account ran, Police Sergeant Moseley Cummins and volunteer Patrolman Robert Ansteth answered a near-riot call which took them to a home in the Kaimuki neighborhood. There they found a Hawaiian boy and his two sisters crouching on a sofa and screaming at the tops of their voices. The mother was also shrieking, and at the same time waving *ti* leaves and sprinkling red Hawaiian salt on the floor to ward off spirits. At ten o'clock that night, she said, her son "detected the odor of ghosts." The spirits, angry at having been discovered, then beat up the boy and tried to strangle his sisters, the mother told the officers. "My husband, who left me, is to blame," she added.

The police attempted to assure the woman that there were no such things as ghosts and assisted the family to the home of the mother's sister. As they left, the harassed mother turned on Sergeant Cummins, "Look," she cried accusingly, "You have goose pimples, too!"

One day in September a rumor flew through the

city. "Saboteurs up Nuuanu Valley." Army observation planes had spotted a large white arrow pointing toward the *pali*. For two consecutive nights the bright moonlight had revealed it shining clearly in the center of a large lawn. It was said to have a number "2" written on it as well as other marks that could not be identified.

The Herbert Dowsetts, long-time residents of Nuuanu, were as interested in the report as anyone else. The following afternoon Mrs. Dowsett was brought out of the house by the roar of a plane that apparently was coming right into her living room. It passed over the house, turned and came back again, flying so low that Mrs. Dowsett thought it was going to hit the roof. Obviously, the pilot was taking a good look by daylight at the Dowsett yacht sail marked "S-2," which they had put out on the grass to sun just two days previously! The Army and Navy are not relaxing, the Dowsetts concluded.

So we all conclude. At any minute of the day you can see planes on inshore patrol off any part of the island, and you know they are patrolling several hundred miles outside, as well. You wake up at daybreak and hear their comforting steady roar overhead.

A few days before the Emperor's last birthday, the rumor spread that a great fleet of Japanese ships was on its way to deliver Oahu to Hirohito for a birthday present. It was interesting to watch each person's reaction as he was told this story. At first, there was a shadow of doubt or fear perhaps, followed almost immediately by a bright expression, then, "Four hundred ships! By God, I just hope they are dumb enough to let that many ships come this far away from home. Boy, what those Army and Navy flyers won't do to them!" But it was too good to be true, everybody agreed, and they were right. The birthdate came and went, but the ships did not appear.

If the Japs come again—and General Emmons has warned us that they will—they are going to find a Hawaii that is not only alert but spoiling for a fight. We were caught napping once, but we believe that this time our planes will be in the air and our ships at sea to meet the enemy. If some Japanese planes should get through, they will not find hangars filled with planes nor runways covered with closely grouped machines. Each plane is now sheltered in an earthwork embankment so that no matter how perfect the attacking pilot's aim, he can damage but one plane with a single bomb. As you drive past Hickam, Wheeler, or any of the many new airfields that have been built in recent months, you never see a plane unless it is landing or taking off. We do not know how many planes are protecting the islands, but since there were four hundred and seventy-five on December 7th, 1941, in Hawaii we believe that the Japs had better bring twenty-five aircraft carriers if they want to match us plane for plane in the air.

Better warships—and more of them—will meet attackers off shore. Only one of our combat battleships, the twenty-six thousand ton *Arizona* was reduced to a total loss in the blitz.*All of the others have been repaired or replaced. The repaired warships are bristling with armaments of the latest design. The cruisers carry the equipment of the newest ships of their class—the heavy cruisers support nine eight-inch guns, the light cruisers fifteen six-inch guns. Below decks, the stern is converted into a compact airplane hangar. A sliding deck moves forward at the touch of a button, bringing out three scouting planes, wings folded. They can be rolled out and catapulted into the air in five minutes. Similar improvements have been made on the ships of all classes, from battleships on down to mosquito boats.

"But suppose that the Japs break through the outer ring? They did it once."

We in Hawaii do not believe they will, but Admiral Nimitz and General Emmons are not taking the layman's view. No matter where an enemy lands on

*See Chapter XIV: Historical Notes.

Oahu, he will meet a murderous barrage of fire. From Diamond Head to Waianae, the artillery of concealed forts—Ruger, DeRussy, Kamehameha, Shafter, and more—cover every inch of ocean and beach. When they open up with big cannon, five-inch anti-aircraft guns, and nine, twelve, and sixteen-inch rifles, the whole end of the island shakes as if in violent earthquake.

The northwest end of the island, where strategists have said the only successful attack could possibly come, offers the island's single open coast. It is flanked on one side by the Waianae mountains, on the other by the Koolau range. If Jap landing barges do succeed in passing our bombers and the ships of our Navy, from the Koolau and the Waianae they would meet the converging fire of the American equivalents of the vicious French Seventy-fives, as well as .50 caliber machine guns, cannon, and howitzers. And if they get by these, still further back, they will run into the savage fire of row upon row of field guns, 240 millimeter guns, big rifles, and more howitzers.

If the enemy characteristically ignores the obvious entry and sends his barges to another part of the island, he will run into barbed wire and barricades and the withering fire of machine guns. All around the island, American soldiers are on guard in pillboxes that stud the beaches and lie concealed in the wide green lawns of expansive estates. Our boys are ready and eager to open up with their 37 millimeter guns. Backing them up are hidden artillery emplacements, bristling with swivel guns covering every approach to possible invasion points. And behind that line are some of the roughest, toughest soldiers in the mid-Pacific, in dugout and armed nests which they have hewn out of the solid lava-rock mountain sides. They command a bird's eye view of the beaches three thousand feet below, of the plateaus where parachute troops might land, and of the deep ravines and gorges into which enemy battalions might disappear.

The Army's job is to defend Pearl Harbor. The Navy's job is to carry the war to the enemy. Pearl Harbor has always been our most powerful Naval base. It contains fifteen thousand linear feet of berthing, its own railroad and immense ammunition depot, dry docks, oil tanks, marine railway and shops, a submarine base, radio center, a fleet air base, batteries of twelve to sixteen-inch guns, and fifty-eight miles of military roads. Torpedo and bomb-sight repair shops have been built, and mammoth fuel tanks are sunk underground, where they were untouched by the bombing on December 7th. Day and night shifts of workers repair and build, repair and build inside the harbor—which is surrounded by a barbed-wire mounted steel fence and commanded by ever-alert gunners in lookout towers.

The morale of the workers is high. They feel themselves a part of a tremendous battle action, swiftly growing and seeking the attack. When our American raiders came in from their Marshall and Gilbert Island attack, defense workers lined the banks of the harbor and cheered the returning heroes. And when the pall-covered stretchers bearing the dead were carried in, the workers stood, hats in hand, silently dedicating themselves to match their own sacrifice with soldiers' sacrifice—to match their work with fighters' tireless hours, their sweat with heroes' blood.

Workers everywhere on the island—at Red Hill, on the various work camps, as well as in the Harbor proper—have become more and more enthusiastic as the deeds of our fighters in the Coral Sea, Midway, and the Solomons answered the question. "Where is our Navy?" They keep silent on the subject of their work, but they take a very personal pride in delivering ahead of schedule, and in performing production miracles. They have made Hawaii an arsenal of democracy from which, to quote Milton, Japan has heard.

Sonorous metal blowing martial sounds . . .
. . . which . . .
Frightened the reign of chaos and old night.

In Hawaii, confidence has been completely restored. The people know that the sea lanes to our Pacific fighting fronts have been made safe, that our submarines, setting out from Pearl Harbor for Japan three thousand miles away, have reached her very shores, and sunk her ships inside her harbors. The people of Hawaii feel the privilege of living in the Pacific war area, on and near battlefields where our soldiers, sailors, and marines are adding unfading glory to American tradition.

XIII

REMEMBER PEARL HARBOR!

I HAVE HAD MY WISH. I HAVE LIVED HISTORY. THE audacious attack on Pearl Harbor is of world-wide significance. For one thing, it gives us in Hawaii and, I should think, everyone on the mainland United States a new conception of the strength of the Axis Powers. We heard many cock-and-bull stories here about Japanese lack of initiative and imagination— that any ability they possessed was solely imitative. If we had believed some, we would have thought that every ship in the Japanese Navy would fall over on its side if it steamed into rough water. Now we have learned the hard way.

No matter how much we despise the Japanese Naval Command which planned and executed one of the most treacherous and despicable stabs in the back ever given any nation, we have to hand it to them. The bold-faced treachery of it surpasses even Hitler's attacks on peaceful nations. But, like Hitler, they delivered the first blow well. If you can forget the ethics of it, you are forced to admit—I will not say admire —the imaginative daring of the attack. For one hour and forty minutes, the Japanese air and naval forces achieved the impossible.*

We in Hawaii were amazed and bewildered when we tried to analyze "how it happened." We refused to dwell on this question. We suppressed vain speculation and awaited the report of the investigating committee. No matter what else that report revealed, it gave implicit testimony to the long-time, skilled planning of the Japanese. Their imperialist and military rulers are desperate but strong.

Japan is not acting alone, but in collaboration with the other members of the Axis. We think she has put her money on the wrong horse. Nevertheless, it is highly significant that she made the Axis her choice to win. We are confident that Japan is wrong, and that the Allies will continue to deal Germany and the Axis crushing blows. But here in Hawaii we have learned that it is important to act as though the thing which we believe cannot happen, may happen.

We hear phrases like "Commit national hara-kiri,"

*See Chapter XIV: Historical Notes.

which suggest that the Japanese have wilfully thrown themselves into this war as a dramatic, desperate, but hopeless gesture to preserve their national honor. But the fact is that she has not committed hara-kiri. Far from it.

We have learned the strength of the Axis, but that knowledge has brought us the blessing of consolidation. Here in Hawaii, as in the whole United States, Pearl Harbor has merged all groups into common action. We had our fascist-minded people, just as the mainland had. We had individuals here who were inclined to do business with Hitler—who did not admire him, perhaps, but who envied him his lack of labor problems. We had our America Firsters. They, like their friends in the States, joined in the clamor of indignation that rose against the attackers.

Since feeling the muscle of the Axis, we feel much nearer to the war. We had a taste of blitzkrieg. The Nazi-Fascist technique hit us. The physical parallels between the attack on us and those on German-occupied countries reminded us directly of other parallels between Japan and the Axis. Before that Sunday, we believed our books and the accounts of our foreign correspondents, but we paid little attention to them. They told us of Japan's suppression of "dangerous" thoughts, her expulsion of university professors, her re-writing of standard history according to the fascist pattern, and her persecution of foreign students for liberalism. I myself have traveled in Japan and been followed by her agents. Many of us here have; but until Pearl Harbor, we only laughed at the naiveté of the Japanese.

Now, no matter how we hate and despise the Japanese imperialists, just as we hate those who paid Hitler, we no longer say they are naive, any more than Hitler is naive. Japan's imperialists see clearly what they must do at home and abroad in order to survive. At home, they have probably succeeded. It seems—and we should act as if it were true—that the fascist mind has completely dominated the population. We have even less hope of a revolution in Japan than in Germany.

Japan claims that there were "suicide" aviators in the attack on Pearl Harbor. Our Navy does not think so. Two "suicide submarines" were captured. It is believed that these small craft were launched some two hundred miles from Pearl Harbor. The Tokyo radio insists proudly that the entire attacking force was an immense mass suicide squadron.* We do not have to condescend to believe the Tokyo radio in order to grant that the Japanese rulers have achieved

*See Chapter XIV: Historical Notes.

a temporary blind obedience to them and to the Emperor that is exceedingly dangerous to us.

What kind of conditioning would make a suicide submarine operator lie alone in the dark caverns of the sea, waiting an opportunity to die in the muck of the ocean? What produces such fanatic loyalty to the Emperor and to the ruling class which he represents? We cannot help asking ourselves these questions. In the answer to them we seek some explanation of the attack.

Groping for these answers, we come with a fresh mind to the old facts which we had let go in one ear and out the other. We recall the want and poverty of the masses of Japan—poverty created by the wholesale appropriation of the nation's wealth and resources into the greedy hands of the five families: the Mitsuis, the Mitsubishis, and the rest. We remember how children are taught superstitious loyalty to the Big Five's friend, Hirohito. How truth is kept from school children from the time they are three years old. How they were never encouraged, as in our schools, to think for themselves, but trained instead to believe that blind, unquestioning loyalty is the supreme virtue.

If the political, economic, and military leaders of Japan had solved Japan's social problem, given Japan's people food, they would not have had to give them fanaticism and superstition. We knew this before, and some had heard it until they were bored, but on that terrible Sunday morning we realized with a jolt that Japan and the Axis will, if they can, impose this intellectual and social blitzkrieg upon us by a blitzkrieg of arms.

It enrages us to reflect that we have permitted some in our midst to prepare Japan for the blitz with which she struck us. Our women and children were killed by scrap-metals which the vast majority of Americans never wanted to go to Japan in the first place. The terrific irony of it, the coldblooded money policy that dictated it, are too much for the most patient to bear. We think it still smells to high heaven, and we spit when we hear the word *appeaser*. If any are left in the State Department, we in Hawaii want them cleaned out!

Right now, when we say "Remember Pearl Harbor!" we are thinking of preparation and war. We are thinking of immediate defense of our actual lives. We are thinking, too, of what makes life worth living in America and why we are willing to die rather than surrender what we have gained in the past two hundred years. We are so convinced of the rightness of the fundamental conception of democracy that we hardly stop to think of it in concrete terms. But we know that it is on the basis of hundreds of pictures of democracy in action every day of our lives that we act now, intuitively, to defend it.

Each of us has his own picture of what it is he is defending. I think at once of Greenfield, Tennessee, the small town where I spent my formative years. Greenfield had a lot of democracy. There was not a home in the town that I, as a growing boy, did not feel welcome to enter and sit down to a meal. I knew the shape and texture of each housewife's biscuits— how Mrs. Lett's always had brown spots of baking powder in them, how Mrs. Hanaway's were small and white. . . . Mrs. MacReady made her own ketchup, spicy and red.

I never knew what it was to feel that someone was "better" than I. Some were stronger, handsomer, brighter, but no Greenfielder would have understood what is meant by class differences. My father probably never made over 150 dollars a month in his life, yet he was one of the town's leading citizens, and I have always been proud of him. I mowed lawns and knew everyone well. They all praised me when I worked hard, and complained if I failed to pull the weeds.

In school I had a square deal. The first year I played

football I was accepted as a man by the older fellows who sat on the curb in front of Brasfield's Drug Store every Sunday. Later, at Vanderbilt University, I ran the campus pool room, yet I belonged to a fraternity, went to the dances, and had sorority dates every week. My professors encouraged independent thinking. I sat up nights concocting ways to confound "Eddie" Mims and "Cocky" Sanborn and got A's and B's for being a good fighter. I encountered broadmindedness more often than meanness.

In my profession too, I have had a square deal. We have a small university here in Hawaii—small enough still that every professor knows the president. We do not have a teachers' union, because not enough professors feel that they need it. Whenever some of us decide that we want one enough to work for it, we can have it. In the meantime, we talk things over with the president.

Before I had written a book, I suspected that getting a manuscript accepted probably depended upon pulling strings, getting a good agent, meeting somebody who would introduce me to somebody. I wrote a book, sent it to two publishers who rejected it for what appeared to be sensible reasons. I sent it to a third, who took it. I wrote another book, which I showed to publishers in New York. Those who rejected it talked about the manuscript in such detail that I felt convinced they had considered it carefully and had formed their decision on the basis of the book alone.

My attitude towards the publishers was perhaps naive but my faith in the democracy that exists in America was so renewed that I felt inspired. "If I can write a good book, I can get it published," I thought. That conviction helped me re-write my book. When I finished, the second publisher who saw it took it.

These pictures are in the back of my mind when I hear or read or think "democracy." In the minds of Americans everywhere there are thousands of similar pictures. Each seems trivial, but put together they add up to some mighty impressive facts—the fact of equality of opportunity and the fact of freedom. These are what democracy means to me.

I am no Pollyanna. I know that there are far too many people in the United States who have not experienced freedom and equality of opportunity to the same degree that I have. If I thought that after this war America was going to be dominated by men of autocratic mind, I would feel weary and spiritless indeed. I believe that when we have dealt the most powerful autocrats in the world their death blow, we will have an easier time of it with those lesser ones at home. I believe that we will learn—have already learned—from the mistakes of the autocrat-ridden Axis countries. We want not only to preserve our democratic institutions, but to extend democracy— even to the shores of Japan.

The treachery, frightfulness, and ruthlessness of the attack on Pearl Harbor springs from a social system in desperation. A healthy social system does not arm for, nor launch, wars of conquest and acquisition. It does not rear men who will strafe ambulances and civilians in the streets. . . .

When the peace comes, remembering Pearl Harbor will mean remembering the tubercular-ridden, under-fed fanatics of Japan, bred by cruelly unjust social relationships. It will mean seeing to it that more equality of opportunity exists in America. It will mean making certain that the people in every country will be allowed to provide for their own livelihood. It will mean permitting these people to set up forms of government that will render fascism and its consequences impossible. Then, not only in war but in peace, will we

REMEMBER PEARL HARBOR!

AMERICAN AND JAPANESE LOSSES

From official Navy release, December 7th, 1942

"ON THE MORNING OF DECEMBER 7, 1941, JAPANESE aircraft temporarily disabled every battleship and most of the aircraft in the Hawaiian area. Other naval vessels, both combatant and auxiliary, were put out of action, and certain shore facilities, especially at the Naval Air Stations, Ford Island, and Kaneohe Bay, were damaged. Most of these ships are now back with the Fleet. The aircraft were all replaced within a few days, and interference with facilities was generally limited to a matter of hours.

"As a result of the Japanese attack, five battleships, the *Arizona, Oklahoma, California, Nevada* and *West Virginia*; three destroyers, the *Shaw, Cassin* and *Downes*; the minelayer *Oglala*; the target ship *Utah*, and a large floating drydock were either sunk or damaged so severely that they would serve no military purposes for some time. In addition, three battleships, the *Pennsylvania*, *Maryland* and *Tennessee*, three cruisers, the *Helena*, *Honolulu*, and *Raleigh*, the seaplane tender *Curtiss*, and the repair ship *Vestal* were damaged.

"Of the 19 Naval vessels listed above as sunk or damaged, the 26-year old battleship *Arizona* will be the only one permanently and totally lost. Preparations for the righting of the *Oklahoma* are now in process, although final decision as to the wisdom of accomplishing this work at this time has not been made. The main and auxiliary machinery, approximately 50 percent of the value, of the *Cassin* and *Downes* were saved. The other 15 vessels either have been or will be salvaged and repaired.

The eight vessels described in the second sentence of paragraph two returned to the Fleet months ago. A number of the vessels described in the first sentence of paragraph two are now in full service, but certain others, which required extensive machinery and intricate electrical overhauling as well as refloating and hull repairing, are not yet ready for battle action. Naval repair yards are taking advantage of these inherent delays to install numerous modernization features and improvements. To designate these vessels by name now would give the enemy information vital to his war plans; similar information regarding enemy ships which our forces have subsequently damaged but not destroyed is denied to us.

"Eighty Naval aircraft of all types were destroyed by the enemy. In addition, the Army lost 97 planes on Hickam and Wheeler Fields. Of these 23 were bombers, 66 were fighters, and 8 were other types.

The most serious American losses were in personnel. As result of the raid on December 7, 1941, 2117 officers and enlisted men of the Navy and Marine Corps were killed, 960 are still reported as missing and 876 were wounded but survived. The Army casualties were as follows: 226 officers and enlisted men were killed or later died of wounds; 396 were wounded, most of whom have now recovered and have returned to duty.

"It is difficult to determine the total number of enemy aircraft participating in the raid, but careful analysis of all reports makes it possible to estimate the number as 21 torpedo planes, 48 dive dombers and 36 horizontal bombers, totalling 105 of all types. Undoubtedly certain fighter planes also were present but these are not distinguished by types and are included in the above figures.

"The enemy lost 28 aircraft due to Navy action,

and the few Army pursuit planes that were able to take off shot down more than twenty Japanese planes. In addition, three submarines, of 45 tons each, were accounted for."

XIV HISTORICAL NOTES
by Daniel Martinez

CHAPTER 1: THIS IS HONOLULU

Page 2:   Editor's note.

In 1941, the military authorities believed, and the general public perceived, that the Japanese carrier forces attacked from the north as well as the south. Actually, the planes were launched that morning from the north at a distance of 220 miles. The first wave of 183 planes concentrated off Kahuku Point and proceeded along three separate routes: down the center of the island, along the west side of the Waianae coastline, and on the northeast side of the Koolau coastline toward Kaneohe Naval Air Station. The map shown here was widely distributed and published during the war years and after. Even to this day, it appears in publications about Pearl Harbor leading to continued misconceptions of how the attack was carried out.

Page 3:   Richard Halliburton, 1900-1939, was an American explorer and writer. His journeys took him to Tibet and up the slopes of Mt. Fujiyama. He flew around the world in his own plane in 1931-32, and was lost at sea in 1939 when the Chinese junk he was sailing from the Orient to San Francisco sank in a typhoon.

Webster's American Biographies.

Page 7:   Saburo Kurusu was appointed "special envoy" to Washington, in an effort to assist Ambassador Nomura in diplomatic negotiations with Secretary of State Cordell Hull.

Gordon Prange, *At Dawn We Slept* (New York, McGraw-Hill, 1981), pp. 357-359 (cited hereafter as *At Dawn We Slept*).

Page 9: Admiral Isaac Kidd was killed near the bridge of the U.S.S. *Arizona*. He was awarded the Medal of Honor.

At Dawn We Slept, p. 513.

Page 11: Damage to the City of Honolulu amounted to $500,000. Hawaiian Department specialists from the U.S. Army found that of the 44 projectiles that landed in the city, all but one were improperly fused anti-aircraft rounds fired by U.S. forces.

Michael Slackman, *Historic Resource Study, U.S.S.* Arizona *Memorial* (Honolulu, Hawaii, National Park Service, 1984), p. 328 (cited hereafter as *H.R.S.*).

Chapter 2: The Attack Begins

Page 19: Editor's note.
Hawaiian word for loin cloth.

Page 19: This perhaps is an oversimplification of fact. In February 1941, Major General Frederick L. Martin and Admiral Patrick N.L. Bellinger, Jr. prepared a paper, commonly referred to as the Martin-Bellinger Report, as to the capability of the Japanese Navy attacking Pearl Harbor. In fairness, however, air patrols recommended in the Martin-Bellinger report were materially impossible. There simply were not enough patrol planes to provide 360-degree searches. Further, Washington was less than candid with Admiral Kimmel and General Short as to the status of military and diplomatic affairs in the Pacific; that is, "Magic" intercepts, the breaking of the Japanese diplomatic code.

At Dawn We Slept, pp. 91-97.

Page 22: Involved in this incident was a PBY (Navy patrol aircraft) from Patrol Wing Two, which also radioed its report. Admiral Kimmel was notified. He was "not all certain that this was a real attack." There had been many false reports prior to this incident. Most damaging was the Navy's failure to notify the Army of the incident. The Army was charged with air protection of the Pacific Fleet.

At Dawn We Slept, pp. 496-497.

Page 23: Radar displayed blips on a screen. The radar is not a listening device but rather an instrument that sends out radio waves and picks them up after they have been reflected by objects such as airplanes. It could determine distance and direction.

Walter Lord, *Day of Infamy* (New York, Holt, Rhinehart & Winston, Inc., 1957), pp. 44-49 (cited hereafter as *Day of Infamy).*

Page 25: The man was Lt. Kermit Tyler, and it was his second day on the job at the Information Center at Fort Shafter. The planes were B-17 bombers that had taken off from Hamilton Field, north of San Francisco on December 6, 1941.

Day of Infamy, pp. 44-49.

Page 25: The Japanese employed six of their finest and largest carriers in the Hawaii Operation: *Agagi, Kaga, Soryu, Hiryu, Zuikaku* and *Shokaku.*

H.R.S., p. 33.

Chapter 3: At the Flying Fields

Page 30: Kaneohe Naval Air Station was the first base

attacked that morning at 7:48 a.m. Japanese fighters and dive bombers swept in and struck 33 PBY patrol planes stationed there. Twenty-seven were destroyed and six damaged.

At Dawn We Slept, pp. 519-533.

Page 36: Lt. Fusata Iida, from the carrier *Soryu,* led the fighter group that attacked Kaneohe Naval Air Station. His plane was damaged in the assault. In keeping with an earlier promise he had made on his carrier, if his aircraft were damaged to the point of no return, he would plunge his plane into the enemy. The pilot, who loved American baseball, was faithful to his promise.

At Dawn We Slept, p. 533.

Page 40: On the day of the attack, there were 20 fighter planes there, 12 of which were P-40's. Several were damaged or destroyed. Five men were killed and nine wounded.

At Dawn We Slept, p. 533.

Page 41: At the time of the attack, none of the carrier aircraft used by the Japanese employed a mustard-yellow paint scheme.

Donald Thorpe, *Japanese Naval Wings* (Fallbrook, CA, Aero Publications, 1968).

Page 45: Lieutenants Welch and Taylor took off from Haleiwa auxiliary field, where they were temporarily assigned for aerial gunnery practice.

At Dawn We Slept, pp. 533-534.

Page 59: Editor's note.
On December 7, 1984, these three individuals' fami-

lies were awarded Purple Hearts aboard the U.S.S. *Arizona* Memorial in a ceremony conducted by the National Park Service.

Page 60:   The explosions that rocked Hickam that morning did inflict heavy damage. It was not, however, as dramatic as described here. The building mentioned was the new Hale Makai. A bomb struck the mess hall section, killing 35 and wounding many. Severe strafing pockmarked the building, the scars of which can still be seen on the walls of the structure today.

Captain Kevin Krejcarek, *Hickam: The 50 Years* (Hickam Air Base, U.S. Air Force, 1985).

Page 63:   Led by Major Truman Landon, this was a flight of B-17's from California.

Day of Infamy, p. 109.

Chapter 4: At Pearl Harbor

Page 68:   There were two waves of Japanese carrier aircraft launched in the attack. The first wave was launched at 6 a.m. and consisted of 183 planes. The second wave flew aloft at 7 a.m. with 167 aircraft employed.

H.R.S., p. 112.

Page 68:   Editor's note.
A closer look at the Pacific Fleet at Pearl Harbor reveals that there were about 135 ships in the harbor. This included warships and assorted yardcraft.

Page 69:   Battleship Row consisted of seven battleships stretching over seven-eighths of a mile along the east side of Ford Island. Respectively, from north to south, they were the U.S.S. *Nevada* (BB-36), U.S.S. *Arizona* (BB-39, inboard), U.S.S. *Vestal* (AR-4, outboard), U.S.S. *Tennessee* (BB-43, inboard), U.S.S. *West Virginia* (BB-48, outboard), U.S.S. *Maryland* (BB-46, inboard), U.S.S. *Oklahoma* (BB-37, outboard), U.S.S. *Neosho* (AO-23 oiler) and U.S.S. *California* (BB-44).

Ray Emory, *Map of Pearl Harbor*, Nov. 22, 1971 (cited hereafter as Emory Map). Note: Mr. Emory is a Pearl Harbor survivor from the U.S.S. *Honolulu* and a former historian of the Pearl Harbor Survivors Association.

Page 71:   The aerial torpedoes employed in the attack were of a special design, but not for the reasons listed above. The depth of water at Pearl Harbor was only 40 feet. Normally, a torpedo would plunge to a depth of over 100 feet. Japanese technicians modified the torpedo with wooden fins and altered the air speed and altitude of the aircraft, producing deadly results.

At Dawn We Slept, pp. 159-160.

Page 81:   The U.S.S. *Utah* (AG-16) was berthed at Fox 11 on the west side of Ford Island about "midway in Battleship Row." To her stern was the U.S.S. *Tangier* (AV-8) and forward of her bow were the U.S.S. *Raleigh* (CL-7) and the U.S.S. *Detroit* (CL-8).

Emory Map.

Page 82:   Peter Tomich was awarded the Medal of Honor posthumously.

Congressional Medal of Honor: The Names, the Deeds (Forest Ranch, CA, Sharp & Dunnigan, 1984), p. 460 (cited hereafter as *Medal of Honor*).

Page 85: The U.S.S. *Nevada,* in the true sense of the words, never "cleared the channel," but rather was run aground to prevent her from sinking and blocking the channel. Further, it was decided to move the *Nevada* across to Waipio Point to lessen her chance of obstructing the harbor.

At Dawn We Slept, pp. 535-536.

Page 85: The black mess attendant was Doris Miller. He won a Naval Cross for his action that day.

H.R.S., p. 149.

Page 86: Captain Bennion (Medal of Honor winner) did not die in this manner. He was removed from the bridge by Doris Miller and others as the flames increased. He eventually was hauled up to the navigation bridge where he died as he was attended by Chief Pharmacist Mate Leak.

H.R.S., pp. 148-149.

Page 89: The *Arizona* was lost when an armor-piercing bomb struck near the forecastle. It plummeted into the forward magazines and ignited a chain-reaction explosion. After the attack, the gratings were examined in the smoke stack area, but no evidence of a bomb piercing here and igniting her magazines in that manner was found.

Arnold Lott and Robert Sumrall, *Ship's Data #3 USS Arizona* (Annapolis, MD, Leeward Publications, 1978) (cited hereafter as *Ship's Data #3).*

Page 92: Commander Fuqua was awarded the Medal of Honor for his actions that day.

Medal of Honor, p. 322.

Page 94:   Commander Cassin Young was awarded the Medal of Honor.

Medal of Honor, p. 488.

Page 95:   In order to save the ship from sinking from a serious bomb hit in her stern, Commander Young beached her on Aiea shoals.

H.R.S., p. 166.

Page 95:   The *Solace* was actually moored one-quarter mile away from the stern of the U.S.S. *Arizona's* starboard side. Moreover, she did not move past the *Arizona* but actually farther away, from berth X-4 to berth X-13 near the U.S.S. *Dobbin.*

Emory Map.

Page 96:   The ship was the U.S.S. *New Orleans.*

Day of Infamy, p. 144.

Page 97:   The aircraft were from the carrier U.S.S. *Enterprise.*

At Dawn We Slept, p. 520.

Page 105:   The author may have confused this ship with U.S.S. *Monaghan,* whose experience was very similar to the action described.

Report of Pearl Harbor Action, U.S.S. Aylwin. Jan. 4, 1942. U.S.S. *Arizona* Memorial, National Park Service Archives.

Chapter 5: Some Noncombatants

Page 114:   Editor's note.
This incredible event was depicted vividly in 20th Century Fox's film, "TORA! TORA! TORA!"

Chapter 6: The Wounded

Page 147: The numbers of wounded flooded and taxed Honolulu's medical facilities. The final statistics of those wounded are: Navy, 710; Marine, 69; Army, 364; and civilian, 35. The total number of wounded was 1,178.

H.R.S., p. 468.

Chapter 7: The Blood Bank

Page 156: The ship was the *Jagersfontein*, inbound from the West Coast. In fact, she was the first of the Allies to join the war. Since Holland was already at war, she had guns aboard and subsequently pulled off the canvas covers and opened up, joining the fight.

Day of Infamy, p. 157.

Chapter 8: The Rescue

Page 162: The plane was one of six from the U.S.S. *Enterprise* that arrived over the harbor at 9 p.m. All six planes were lost, with three pilots killed and two wounded.

H.R.S., pp. 299-303.

Chapter 9: The Dead

Page 172: Mr. Harlan Gray, in an oral history interview, recalled the burials at Red Hill. He told of the use of steam shovels to dig burial trenches for hundreds of dead. Mr. Gray was a foreman on the Red Hill underground oil storage project for the Navy.

U.S.S. Arizona *Memorial National Park Service Oral History Collection.*

Page 173:   The death toll that day reached 2,403. The statistics
speak for themselves: Navy, 2,008 (1,177 from the
U.S.S. *Arizona*); Marine, 109; Army, 218; and
civilian, 68.

H.R.S., p. 468.

Chapter 10: The Japanese Community

Page 189:   It is significant to note that young Japanese-American males, in an effort to prove their loyalty and
love for the land of their birth, enlisted in large
numbers in the 100th Infantry Battalion and, later,
the 442nd Regimental Combat Team. The 442nd
was the most decorated regiment of World War II.
Among the laurels of sacrifice were more than
18,143 decorations, half of which were Purple
Hearts.

H.R.S., p. 368.

Chapter 11: The Niihau Story

Page 195:   The planes were Mitsubishi A6M2, Type 21, Zero
fighter.

H.R.S., p. 318.

Page 212:   This catch phrase has become an enduring myth in
Hawaii. The facts, as they have recently been
brought to light, show that Ben Kanahele was shot
only twice, according to the medical treatment
records at Waimea Hospital, case #8934.

Burl Burlingame, "Mystery Fighter: The Bizarre
Battle of Niihau Island," *Honolulu Star-Bulletin*,
Dec. 6-9, 1986.

Chapter 12: A Year After

Page 228: Editor's note.
On October 24, 1944, martial law ended in Hawaii. It had lasted more than three years, one of the longest ever enacted in any territory or state in U.S. history.

Page 234: The *Arizona* weighed over 32,000 tons and is one of two vessels present at the time of the attack that still rest at Pearl Harbor. The other is the U.S.S. *Utah*. The U.S.S. *Oklahoma* was salvaged and sold for scrap. On her way to a West Coast scrap yard in 1947, she sank in a storm, 540 miles northeast of Pearl Harbor. Those three vessels never saw service again.

Ships' Battle Reports & Histories, U.S.S. *Arizona* Memorial Archives, National Park Service.

Chapter 13: Remember Pearl Harbor

Page 242: Editor's note.
This carrier air assault brought about a new era of naval warfare. In 1941, the admirals of the world, who believed in battleships as the weapon that would decide naval engagements, saw that belief founder after Pearl Harbor.

Page 244: Editor's note.
Clearly, the author's perceptions were correct. Japan never intended to initiate her attack on Pearl Harbor with suicide squadrons. It was not until 1944 that the Japanese, desperate to save their homeland, used this extreme measure.

About Daniel Martinez

Daniel Martinez, son of a registered nurse and an aerospace staff programmer for TRW Systems, was born in Long Beach, California. He spent his youth in Los Angeles, where he attended California State University at Dominquez Hills. He won the Jack Kilfoil History Scholarship and was named in *Who's Who Among University and College Students* in 1979. He graduated with a bachelor's degree in American history and is currently finishing his master's degree in public history and historic preservation.

Mr. Martinez co-authored *Centennial Observance: The 100th Year Anniversary of the Battle of the Little Big Horn* and *The Reno-Benteen Entrenchment Trail* (Custer Battlefield National Monument, National Park Service). He currently is working on two publications, a pictorial essay on the Pearl Harbor attack and a history of the U.S.S. *Utah*. He is now employed as a park ranger/interpretive specialist for the National Park Service at the U.S.S. *Arizona* Memorial, Hawaii.

TALES OF THE PACIFIC

JACK LONDON

Stories of Hawaii by Jack London
Thirteen yarns drawn from the famous author's love affair
with Hawaii Nei.
$4.95   ISBN 0-935180-08-7

The Mutiny of the "Elsinore," by Jack London
Based on a voyage around Cape Horn in a windjammer
from New York to Seattle in 1913, this romance between
the lone passenger and the captain's daughter reveals
London at his most fertile and fluent best. The lovers are
forced to outface a rioting band of seagoing gangsters in
the South Pacific.
$4.95   ISBN 0-935180-40-0

Captain David Grief by Jack London
Captain David Grief, South Sea tycoon, came to the
Pacific at the age of twenty, and two decades later he protected a vast trading empire. Eight long tales of daring and
adventure by the famous American storyteller who did
some of his best writing in that region.
$3.95   ISBN 0-935180-34-6

South Sea Tales by Jack London
Fiction from the violent days of the early century, set
among the atolls of French Oceania and the high islands of
Samoa, Fiji, Pitcairn, and "the terrible Solomons."
$4.95   ISBN 0-935180-14-1

HAWAII

A Hawaiian Reader
Thirty-seven selections from the literature of the past
hundred years including such writers as Mark Twain,
Robert Louis Stevenson and James Jones.
$4.95   ISBN 0-935180-07-9

The Spell of Hawaii
A companion volume to A Hawaiian Reader. Twenty-four
selections from the exotic literary heritage of the islands.
$4.95   ISBN 0-935180-13-3

Kona by Marjorie Sinclair
The best woman novelist of post-war Hawaii dramatizes
the conflict between a daughter of Old Hawaii and her
straitlaced Yankee husband. Nor is the drama resolved in
their children.
$3.95   ISBN 0-935180-20-6

The Golden Cloak by Antoinette Withington
The romantic story of Hawaii's monarchs and their friends, from Kamehameha the Great, founder of the dynasty, to Liliuokalani, last queen to rule in America's only royal palace.
$3.95   ISBN 0-935180-26-5

Teller of Tales by Eric Knudsen
Son of a pioneer family of Kauai, the author spent most of his life on the Garden Island as a rancher, hunter of wild cattle, lawyer, and legislator. Here are sixty campfire yarns of gods and goddesses, ghosts and heroes, cowboy adventures and legendary feats aong the valleys and peaks of the island.
$4.95   ISBN 0-935180-33-8

The Wild Wind a novel by Marjorie Sinclair
On the Hana Coast of Maui, Lucia Gray, great-granddaughter of a New England missionary, seeks solitude but embarks on an interracial marriage with a Hawaiian cowboy. Then she faces some of the mysteries of the Polynesia of old.
$ 4.95   ISBN 0-935180-3-3

Myths and Legends of Hawaii by Dr. W.D. Westervelt
A broadly inclusive, one-volume collection of folklore by a leading authority. Completely edited and reset format for today's readers of the great prehistoric tales of Maui, Hina, Pele and her fiery family, and a dozen other heroic beings, human or ghostly.
$3.95   ISBN 0-935180-43-5

Claus Spreckles, The Sugar King in Hawaii by Jacob Adler
Sugar was the main economic game in Hawaii a century ago, and the boldest player was Claus Spreckels, a California tycoon who built a second empire in the Islands by ruthless and often dubious means.
$3.95   ISBN 0-935180-76-1

Remember Pearl Harbor by Blake Clark
An up-to-date edition of the first full-length account of the effect of the December 7, 1941 "blitz" that precipitated America's entrance into World War II and is still remembered vividly by military and civilian survivors of the airborne Japanese holocaust.
$3.95   ISBN 0-935180-49-4

Russian Flag Over Hawaii: The Mission of Jeffery Tolamy, a novel by Darwin Teilhet
A vigorous adventure novel in which a young American struggles to unshackle the grip held by Russian filibusters on the Kingdom of Kauai. Kamehameha the Great and many other historical figures play their roles in a colorful love story.
$3.95   ISBN 0-935180-28-1

The Betrayal of Liliuokalani: Last Queen of Hawaii 1838-1917 by Helena G. Allen
A woman caught in the turbulent maelstrom of cultures in conflict. Treating Liliuokalani's life with authority, accuracy and details, *Betrayal* also is a tremendously informative concerning the entire period of missionary activity and foreign encroachment in the islands.
$6.95   ISBN 0-935180-89-3

Rape in Paradise by Theon Wright
The sensational *"Massie Case"* of the 1930's shattered the tranquil image that mainland U.S.A. had of Hawaii. One woman shouted "Rape!" and the island erupted with such turmoil that for twenty years it was deemed unprepared for statehood. A fascinating case study of race relations and military-civilian relations.
$4.95   ISBN 0-935180-88-5

Hawaii's Story by Hawaii's Queen by Lydia Liliuokalani
The Hawaiian kingdom's last monarch wrote her biography in 1897, the year before the annexation of the Hawaiian islands by the United States. Her story covers six decades of island history told from the viewpoint of a major historical figure.
$6.95   ISBN 0-935180-85-0

The Legends and Myths of Hawaii by David Kalakaua
Political and historical traditions and stories of the pre-Cook period capture the romance of old Polynesia. A rich collection of Hawaiian lore originally presented in 1888 by Hawaii's "merrie monarch."
$6.95   ISBN 0-935180-86-9

Mark Twain in Hawaii: Roughing It in the Sandwich Islands
The noted humorist's account of his 1866 trip to Hawaii at a time when the islands were more for the native than the tourists. The writings first appeared in their present form in Twain's important book. *Roughing It* includes an introductory essay from *Mad About Islands* by A. Grove Day.
$4.95   ISBN 0-935180-93-1

SOUTH SEAS

Best South Sea Stories
Fifteen writers capture all the romance and exotic adventure of the legendary South Pacific including James A. Michener, James Norman Hall, W. Somerset Maugham, and Herman Melville.
$4.95   ISBN 0-935180-12-5

Love in the South Seas by Bengt Danielsson
The noted Swedish anthropologist who served as a member of the famed *Kon-Tiki* expedition here reveals the sex and family life of the Polynesians, based on early accounts as well as his own observations during many years in the South Seas.
$3.95   ISBN 0-935180-25-7

The Trembling of a Leaf by W. Somerset Maugham
Stories of Hawaii and the South Seas, including "Red," the author's most successful story, and "Rain," his most notorious one.
$4.95   ISBN 0-935180-21-4

Rogues of the South Seas by A. Grove Day
Eight true episodes featuring violent figures from Pacific history, such as the German filibuster who attempted to conquer the Hawaiian Islands for the Russian Czar; "Emma, Queen of a Coconut Empire"; and "The Brothers Rorique: Pirates De Luxe." Forward by James A. Michener.
$3.95   ISBN 0-935180-24-9

Horror in Paradise: Grim and Uncanny Tales from Hawaii and the South Seas, edited by A. Grove Day and Bacil F. Kirtley
Thirty-four writers narrate "true" episodes of sorcery and the supernatural, as well as gory events on sea and atoll.
$4.95   ISBN 0-935180-23-0

The Blue of Capricorn by Eugene Burdick
Stories and sketches from Polynesia, Micronesia, and Melanesia by the co-author of *The Ugly American* and *The Ninth Wave*. Burdick's last book explores an ocean world rich in paradox and drama, a modern world of polyglot islanders and primitive savages.
$3.95   ISBN 0-935180-36-2

The Book of Puka Puka by Robert Dean Frisbie
Lone trader on a South Sea atoll, "Ropati" tells charmingly of his first years on Puka-Puka, where he was destined to rear five half-Polynesian children. Special foreword by A. Grove Day.
$3.95   ISBN 0-935180-27-3

Manga Reva by Robert Lee Eskridge
A wandering American painter voyaged to the distant Gambier Group in the South Pacific and, charmed by the life of the people of "The Forgotten Islands" of French Oceania, collected many stories from their past — including the supernatural. Special introduction by Julius Scammon Rodman.
$3.95   ISBN 0-935180-35-4

The Lure of Tahiti selected and edited by A. Grove Day
Fifteen stories and other choice extracts from the rich literature of "the most romantic island in the world." Authors include Jack London, James A. Michener, James Norman Hall, W. Somerset Maugham, Paul Gauguin, Pierre Loti, Herman Melville, William Bligh, and James Cook.
$3.95   ISBN 0-935180-31-1

In Search of Paradise by Paul L. Briand, Jr.
A joint biography of Charles Nordhoff and James Norman Hall, the celebrated collaborators of *Mutiny on the "Bounty"* and a dozen other classics of South Pacific literature. This book, going back to the time when both men flew combat missions on the Western Front in World War I, reveals that the lives of "Nordhoff and Hall" were almost as fascinating as their fiction.
$4.95   ISBN 0-935180-48-6

The Fatal Impact: Captain Cook in the South Pacific by Alan Moorehead
A superb narrative by an outstanding historian of the exploration of the world's greatest ocean — adventure, courage, endurance, and high purpose with unintended but inevitable results for the original inhabitants of the islands.
$3.95   ISBN 0-935180-77-X

The Forgotten One by James Norman Hall
Six "true tales of the South Seas," some of the best stories by the co-author of *Mutiny on the "Bounty."* Most of these selections portray "forgotten ones" — men who sought refuge on out-of-the-world islands of the Pacific.
$3.95   ISBN 0-935180-45-1

Home from the Sea: Robert Louis Stevenson in Samoa, by Richard Bermann
Impressions of the final years of R.L.S. in his mansion, Vailima, in Western Samoa, still writing books, caring for family and friends, and advising Polynesian chieftains in the local civil wars.
$3.95   ISBN 0-935180-75-3

Coronado's Quest: The Discovery of the American Southwest by A. Grove Day

The story of the expedition that first entered the American Southwest in 1540. A pageant of exploration with a cast of dashing men and women — not only Hispanic adventurers and valient Indians of a dozen tribes, but gray-robed friars like Marcos des Niza — as well as Esteban, the black Moorish slave who was slain among the Zuni pueblos he had discovered.

$3.95   ISBN 0-935180-37-0

A Dream of Islands: Voyages of Self-Discovery in the South Seas by A. Gavan Daws

The South Seas . . . the islands of Tahiti, Hawaii, Samoa, the Marquesas . . . the most seductive places on earth, where physically beautiful brown-skinned men and women move through a living dream of great erotic power. *A Dream of Islands* tells the stories of five famous Westerners who found their fate in the islands: John Williams, Herman Melville, Walter Murray Gibson, Robert Louis Stevenson, Paul Gauguin.

$4.95   ISBN 0-935180-71-2

How to Order

Send check or money order with an additional $2.00 for the first book and $1.00 thereafter to cover mailing and handling to:

Mutual Publishing
2055 North King Street, Suite 202, Honolulu, HI 96819

For airmail delivery add $2.00 per book.